HISTORIC  SCOTLAND

EDINBURGH CASTLE

HISTORIC SCOTLAND

EDINBURGH CASTLE

IAIN MACIVOR

B. T. Batsford Ltd/Historic Scotland

© Iain MacIvor 1993
First published 1993
Reprinted 1997

Typeset by Servis Filmsetting Ltd, Manchester
and printed in Great Britain by
The Bath Press, Bath

Published by B.T. Batsford Ltd
583 Fulham Road, London SW6 5BY

A CIP catalogue record for this book is available from
the British Library

ISBN 0 7134 7295 2 (limp)

Contents

Illustrations

Colour plates

Acknowledgements

The author and publishers would like to thank the following for their kind permission to reproduce photographs and illustrations:

16 City of Carlisle. 20 Württemburgische Landesbibliothek, Stuttgart. 23 and 42 Royal Collection © 1993 Her Majesty The Queen. 25 and 62 Trustees of the National Library of Scotland. 28 Trustees of the National Gallery, London. 29 Glasgow Museums: Art Gallery and Museum. 30 His Grace the Duke of Atholl's collection at Blair Castle, Perthshire. 31 Private collection (present location unknown 1993); photograph Courtauld Institute of Art. 32, 37, 38, 51, 59, 69, 70 and 77 National Galleries of Scotland. 35 British Library. 48 British Library. 49 and 83 Trustees of the National Museums of Scotland. 52 Edinburgh City Libraries. 56 National Maritime Museum, London. 64, 75 and 82 Royal Commission on the Ancient and Historical Monuments of Scotland. 74 Royal Incorporation of Architects in Scotland. 84 Trustees of the Scottish National War Memorial. 96 Press Association Ltd.

Colour plates: 1 Patricia and Angus Macdonald. 2 National Galleries of Scotland. 7 Österreichische Nationalbibliothek, Wien. 12 Christie's.

Foreword
by Magnus Magnusson

Edinburgh Castle is not only the most visible and tangible talisman of Edinburgh but also symbolic of so many aspects of Scotland itself: of Scotland past and Scotland present, of Scotland changing and Scotland still.

This book encapsulates, in 40,000 words and over 340 million years, the story of a star attraction in the Scottish firmament: the story of a place *par excellence* which has transmuted from ancient fastness to medieval fortress and from royal residence to garrison barracks to romantic ancient monument.

The narrative brilliantly conveys the tides of changing fortune which have radically altered the functions of the castle over the centuries – and altered our own perceptions of it.

It chronicles, chapter by compelling chapter, the Castle yarn from the earliest evidence of occupation in the Bronze Age, through the stronghold days of the Gododdin feasting before massacre around AD 600, to the first regalities bestowed by Malcolm Canmore and his sainted Queen Margaret, who died there in 1093. Under the Stewarts it became a royal palace, a treasury, a national record repository, an armaments workshop, a gun foundry and chief arsenal of the kingdom. There is no more significant building in Scotland – not least the Great Hall, which is a crux of Renaissance influence in Britain.

Above all, it is the story of a marvellous monument on a par with the Tower of London and the Kremlin of Moscow: a great rock born in a volcanic convulsion on the Equator 340 million years ago, now crowned with one of the most dramatic – and attractive – strongholds in the world.

Introduction

Archaeological excavation has recently shown that Edinburgh's Castle Rock, in origin a glacier-eroded volcano, was being used by man in the Bronze Age, and was substantially settled in the Iron Age when the Romans occupied southern Scotland. A continuing place of strength there seems to be implied in an enigmatic poem of about AD 600, though the interpretation of the poem is a continuing subject of debate. When the kingdom of Scotland took in Lothian, the site began to evolve into an important royal fortress. It was a principal residence of Malcolm III, his Queen Margaret who died there in 1093, and three of their sons who succeeded as kings. The best known of the latter, David I, built St Margaret's Chapel, the earliest surviving structure in the Castle – for the already-ancient stronghold may now be called a feudal castle. Edinburgh was one of the castles given as security to Henry II of England in 1174 for the ransom of the Scottish king, who had been captured in battle. It was besieged and captured by Edward I in 1296 in his first campaign to subdue Scotland to his overlordship, and several times changed hands during the long struggle for independence that followed.

In 1361 David II began ambitious works which continued into the dynasty of the Stewarts, and there are from this time on more structures or fragments of structures remaining today. The Castle played a conspicuous part in the violent domestic politics of the fifteenth century while beginning to develop new roles, and the recognition of the status of the burgh as the chief city of Scotland increased the military significance of the fortress protecting it. By the reigns of James IV and his son James V – 1488 to 1542 – the Castle had reached the zenith of its prestige, as stronghold, palace, arsenal, gun foundry, armaments workshop, treasury and repository of the national records.

At the same time the Castle began to decline as a royal seat because new palaces at the Abbey of Holyrood and elsewhere were more gracious and attractive. When in 1566 Mary Queen of Scots went to the Castle before giving birth there to her child, the prince who was to be James VI of Scotland and James I of England, the choice was made on the grounds of its security and renown, not its amenity. After Mary's enforced abdication, the Castle supported her cause until in the siege of 1573 it was devastated by gunfire into surrender.

The fortifications were remodelled later in that decade and put up a prolonged resistance to the Covenanters in 1640, to Oliver Cromwell ten years later, and to the forces supporting William and Mary during the long defence by the Duke of Gordon in 1689. Shots were last fired in anger in brushes between the Hanoverian garrison and Prince Charles Edward's army occupying the town in 1745. By then the Castle had become purely a military base. The last important work on the Palace within its walls had been for James VI's 'Homecoming' from England in 1617, and his son Charles I was to be the last ruler who stayed there overnight. From the time of Cromwell's occupation ancient structures had been converted for use by the garrison, and after the 1707 Act of Union, which brought the separate realm of Scotland to an end, appreciable numbers of new army buildings were raised. By the end of the eighteenth century they extended over the whole of the western area of the Rock to provide for the principal garrison in Scotland, and they are now a large presence in many views of the stronghold.

Sir Walter Scott helped to foster a new awareness of the Castle as a great national monument, and a sharpened appreciation of it in Victoria's reign led to much activity to try to make its buildings look more romantic. The majestic impact of the place had become a symbol of Scotland, a symbolism emphasized by the decision to locate the Scottish National War Memorial there after the First World War. Gradually the ancient fortress has attracted increasing numbers of visitors, and in the 1980s major schemes were set up to welcome visitors more adequately. One of the schemes was the construction of a tunnel to segregate traffic from visitors inside the Castle, and it was in the course of preliminary archaeological investigation at one end of the tunnel that the first evidence of prehistoric man on the Rock was found.

As might be expected, there is disagreement among scholars on some of the matters relating to history, archaeology and architectural history in the present book, especially in its earlier part, and I have tried to indicate the most significant areas where there are views differing from those that I express here. The latter are put forward, I hope, with an appropriate degree of humility, for through the long gestation of the book I have felt some sense of awe at the spread of the story in time and subject matter, and the task could not have been attempted without the help and encouragement of many friends in all disciplines.

Among them I owe special debts to Dr David Breeze, Dr David Caldwell, the late Professor Gordon Donaldson, John Dunbar, Bent Petersen, Geoffrey Stell and Dr David Walker. On particular aspects, I most gratefully acknowledge my use of the draft report on the 1988–91 excavations kindly lent me by Dr Stephen Driscoll and Peter Yeoman, on which the first part of the book is modelled; much aid on architectural history from Dr Richard Fawcett; an introduction to computers without which the text would not have come together, by Peter Scott; insights into the 'Dark Ages' from Dr Ian Smith; Christopher Tabraham's crucial role as my mentor and provider of the illustrations; and the scene-setting by Dr Colin MacFadyen, the author of the opening geological section. Finally, I would like to thank Joseph White, Historic Scotland's Photographic Librarian.

CHAPTER ONE

Beginnings – the Rock up to AD 1057

Volcano

The rock upon which Edinburgh Castle was built represents the eroded remnants of a volcano which formed over 340 million years ago, early in the geological period known as the Carboniferous. At that time the geography of northern Britain was quite unlike the distribution of land and sea existing today. The environment was also different because Britain was then positioned over the Equator and therefore had a hot tropical climate.

Within what is now the Scottish Midland Valley area during early Carboniferous times there was a constant battle between the land and the sea for supremacy of the landscape. When the sea level fell relative to the land extensive jungle-like forests formed, in which there lived a variety of primitive animals including amphibians, giant-sized insects and the reptile ancestors of the dinosaurs. When the sea level rose, the forests gave way to lagoons and shallow, open tropical seas in which primitive fish and other marine creatures thrived.

Huge quantities of sediment accumulated in this constantly changing Carboniferous landscape, including coal, oil-shale and ironstone, which millions of years later became crucial in the economic development of the Midland Valley. It was into this environment that the volcano which would become Castle Rock was born. The event occurred when great strains developed in the earth's crust enabling hot molten rock (or magma) to rise from the earth's mantle upward to the surface. After an upward journey of between 10 and 20km (6 and 12 miles), the magma forced a passage through the recently accumulated sediments and erupted into the landscape. The first material to be ejected would have been ash, blanketing the area around the newly-formed volcanic vent. Subsequent eruptions would have been of both lavas and ash which, with the passage of time, built up to form a large composite cone volcano. Lavas from the volcano flowed far from the vent, which was connected to the magma source deep beneath ground by a volcanic pipe or conduit. One of these lava flows may be seen today in Holyrood Park, which contains the remains of another volcanic complex related to the Castle Rock volcano. The lavas from the latter were typically hard, dark coloured and fine textured. After several hundred or a few thousand years the Castle Rock volcano became extinct, and lava which was passing up through the volcanic vent became trapped in the pipe, where it cooled.

Millions of years passed and the ageing volcanic edifice was gradually buried beneath new layers of sediment which continued to accumulate throughout the Carboniferous period and later. Eventually the processes of erosion stripped off these layers of sedimentary rock and the remains of the Castle Rock volcano were uncovered. The most recent phase of erosion occurred during the last Ice Age between ten and twenty thousand years ago. The erosive power of the ice not only removed the overlying sediment, and the layers of lava and ash which comprised the cone, but in addition the ice sheet cut away the less resistant older sediment layers below the ground level of the ancient volcano. However, the ice could not reduce the volcano's solid basalt core, representing its feeder pipe or conduit, to the same level as the sediments. As a result, a great rock column was left standing proud in the landscape and represented an obstacle over and around which the ice sheet was compelled to flow. As the ice encountered the basalt from the west it followed three paths. Ice was diverted to the north and south around the obstacle of the basalt column, and as a consequence gouged out a deep horseshoe-shaped hollow in the relatively soft Carboniferous sediment around the column. The gouged areas now correspond to Princes Street Gardens to the north and the King's Stables Road–Grassmarket area to the south. Ice also rose up over the obstacle and slid down the other side to the west. This smoothed the basalt and allowed for the preservation of a wedge of Carboniferous sediment in the wake of Castle Rock. This wedge now corresponds to the Royal Mile. The three streams of ice merged near the site of the palace of Holyroodhouse, where the ice sheet resumed its eastward flow. The geographical feature produced by this ice action is known as 'crag-and-tail', and the Castle Rock–Royal Mile example is perhaps the best example of its kind in existence (**colour plate 4**).

Today the visitor to the Castle Rock can see the cylindrical plug of black basalt, 80m (260ft) high, which 340 million years ago was a molten mass within a volcanic conduit. Excellent exposures of the basalt occur around the base of the Rock and within the Castle limits. On Johnston Terrace, the contact between the basalt-filled conduit and the layered Carboniferous sediments through which the volcano erupted is well displayed. The superb crag-and-tail feature of the Castle Rock and Royal Mile, a legacy of the Ice Age, may be appreciated from many parts of the city.

The end of the tunnel

Man may first have set foot on the Rock around eight thousand years ago, when the archaeological record for the northern parts of Britain shows the appearance of Mesolithic hunters and gatherers. The Rock rose from a landscape covered with a good deal of woodland containing much oak and birch, and which included to the north the boggy ground about the loch fringed with reeds. The basalt towered precipitously above the loch, as it did also over the land on its southern side (**colour plate 5**). An intrepid man might climb the crags, but the ascent could far more simply be made from the east or west. To the east, the tail of the crag-and-tail formation (the Castle Hill of today) gave an easy upward route skirting the steep rocky slopes defining the summit, while to the west there was a scramble among and around masses of rock, leading to the lowest of two west-facing shelves or terraces of ground. A further fairly gentle ascent reached the upper terrace – the point to which the most straightforward route from the east also led. Still higher was the rock-girt summit, its convex form rising to a height of 150m (500ft) above sea level. All of these upper parts of the Rock would have supported a scatter of trees, together with a good grassy cover over large areas.

For a long time it had been conjectured that prehistoric man later occupied this prominent site, which so commands the surrounding area that it is a natural focus for settlement. Confirmation of prehistoric use, however, only came in the late 1980s. The evidence emerged as a consequence of the proposed excavation of the tunnel (with a shop and a restaurant at its ends) which has already been mentioned. Only the middle section of the tunnel was to be bored out of the solid rock. The two ends were to be engineered as 'cut-and-cover' – cutting a big trench and then covering it over with a concrete lid.

As a preliminary, an archaeological excavation was arranged to examine the strips of ground that would be disturbed by the cuts and

1 *The archaeological excavation of 1988 in progress on Mills Mount, in front of the eighteenth-century Cart Shed.*

by the preparation of the adjacent sites for proposed buildings. The cut to the west of the tunnel was to be located beyond and below the high citadel-like summit of the Rock, on the upper of the two broad shelves or terraces of ground already noted, and today called (after a gun battery that was raised there in the sixteenth century) Mills Mount. At such a distance from the summit, the scope for discovery of very early remains might have been reckoned to be limited. Yet Mills Mount, explored between 1988 and the beginning of 1991, threw a narrow and brilliant shaft of light on the story of the Rock in prehistory (**1** and **2**).

At the lowest level of the excavation, the surface of the natural clay had a heavily trampled appearance. The clay contained minute flecks of charcoal, and set upon and cut into its surface were features that included a small area of pebble pavement, a stone-built drain, post-holes, pits and simple hearths. A sample from one of the hearths gave a radiocarbon date estimated at somewhere between 972 and 830 BC, that is to say in the late Bronze Age or early Iron Age. Within the small area examined it was not possible to determine how many buildings were represented: typical houses of that period in south-east Scotland were over 10m (33ft) in diameter, so only fragments could be revealed in the narrow space available for excavation. This small sample of the earliest remains might conceivably represent no more than a cluster of dwellings on the well-drained and quite inviting terrace, exploiting the considerable area of grazing round about. A much more likely interpretation, however, is that the houses belonged to a widely spreading hill-top settlement (maybe enclosed to west and east where the ascent was easy), of the kind that is a notable feature of Lothian during the early first millennium BC.

There may have been a period of abandonment, or at least greatly reduced activity, between this first phase of use of the Rock and the succeeding major phase. The structures of the latter were similar to those that have just been noted, though they were better preserved, more extensive and substantial. There can be little doubt that they were domestic, and although no evidence was found to establish the construction phase of the structures, both radio-

2 *Archaeology and the Tunnel 1988–91: the sites excavated are hatched. The eastern end of the tunnel opened from the Victorian coal yard (1) north of the Gatehouse (2). Its first short length was devised as a cut-and-cover operation, then the line was taken through the solid basalt, under the Forewall Battery (3) and beneath the highest part or 'citadel' of the Rock passing between the apse of the Scottish National War Memorial (4) and St Margaret's Chapel (5) to a point by the Charles II defences (6) where there began a long section of cut-and-cover through Mills Mount (7) and the eighteenth-century Cart Shed (8); its western end opening on to a level area between the northern defences (9) and part of the Scottish United Services Museum (10). The length of the tunnel engineered through the Rock is emphasized on the diagram by broken lines. It was the site at Mills Mount in front of the Cart Shed that afforded the first evidence of prehistoric settlement on the Castle Rock. (Drawing by Dennis Gallagher.)*

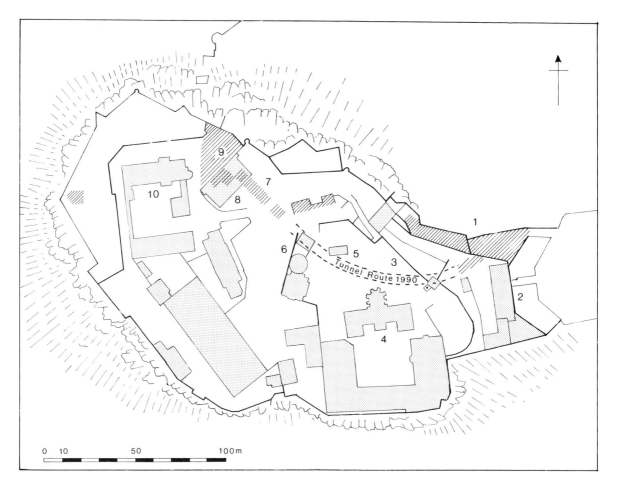

carbon analysis and the testimony of abundant artefacts pointed to a flourishing occupation in the first and second centuries AD (3 and 4). Parts of three houses were identified, and it is most likely that the features represent elements of the interior of a hillfort – such later prehistoric settlements are widespread throughout southeast Scotland. Two large ditches identified in one of the other excavated areas, to the east of the Rock, used as part of the defences of the medieval castle, may possibly have been first cut in the late Iron Age.

The most striking body of artefacts, as well as the most informative in terms of date, is the wealth of Roman material recovered, including pottery and bronzes. The ornaments include several brooches (5) and it has been commented that the range of pottery, both ordinary wares and the fine red vessels called samian ware, might not have been out of place in a fort on the Antonine Wall. The material must represent close contact and commerce with the Roman military in the region. It extends in date from the later first century, the period of the Roman advance into north Britain under Julius Agricola, through the middle decades of the second century when the Roman army again moved north and began to construct the Antonine Wall in AD 142–3 as a new frontier. The material, however, did not contain anything significant from the third century – nothing to correspond with the short-lived invasion by the Emperor Severus that established a nearby Roman supply base at Cramond.

Mention of objects associated with the Roman military presence raises the question of the relationship of the Iron Age archaeology of the Rock to a political background. The implications of the results of the excavation to an already complicated pattern are still being considered, though the elements of a tentative outline have been known for a long time. Following the evidence of Ptolemy's geographical work written in the second century AD, it has been accepted that part of Britain southward from the Forth and centred on Lothian was the territory of the tribe that Ptolemy names ’Ωταδινοι (he is the sole primary source for the name), Latinized as *Votadini*. The tribe later appears in literature in its own British or Old Welsh tongue as, among other spellings, the *Gododdin*. It is uncertain how far its territory extended from Lothian towards the English Tyne; along the Forth, the Votadini bordered with the tribes that were to be recognized by classical authors as Picts, a grouping that seems to have been continually hostile to the power and influence of the Roman Empire in north Britain.

3 *Reconstruction of the rock in the late Iron Age (first and second centuries AD). (Drawing by Jim Proudfoot.)*

4 *Reconstruction of the late Iron Age houses identified in the excavation. (Drawing by David Simon.)*

By contrast, it has been conjectured that the Votadini were more friendly to, or even allies of, Rome, and the abundance of Roman objects found on the Rock in the 1988–91 excavation may well give added weight to the idea. At the same time it confirms a high importance in this epoch to the place that was to become Edinburgh Castle, an importance that may run alongside that of Traprain Law, hitherto seen as the single chief place of the Votadini.

The domestic occupation revealed in the first two phases of the archaeology of Mills Mount prompts the reasonable assumption that, with these habitations near the Rock's perimeter, the citadel-like summit would also be occupied, amounting to an extensive area for the late Iron Age community. The third phase of the archaeology of Mills Mount was very different. The buildings of the late Iron Age were abandoned, and all their features were sealed by extensive layers of dumped house rubbish, rich in discarded artefacts, layers which may have taken centuries to accumulate. Some parts of this midden were almost pure hearth sweepings, some were decayed residues of matted straw which might have been thatch, bedding or floor covering. It may be inferred that, while the Mills Mount site was virtually abandoned, occupation must have continued with some intensity elsewhere to produce such an amount of rubbish. This occupation was possibly adjacent to the limited area of excavation, or alternatively on and around the summit. Whichever interpretation is right, this long-continuing midden, burrowed by rodents, provides a clue pointing to some continuity of settlement on the Rock from the late Iron Age up to and through the early medieval period.

5 *Roman period brooches found in the excavation.* (Above left), *a trumpet brooch which may have been made in the later first or early second century* AD. (Below left), *a dragonesque brooch of a type which was produced between around* AD 50 *and* 150.

6 *The war-band of King Mynyddog leaves Din Eidyn: the image of life on the Rock given by the bard Aneirin. (Drawing by David Simon.)*

His drinking horn was handsome in the hall of
   Eidyn,
His kingliness was spectacular, his mead was
   intoxicating.
(Translation by Kenneth H. Jackson.)

Within the continuity, however, there are archaeological hints that the character of the settlement was changing after direct or indirect Roman influence in the region tailed off. While patterns of any kind may not be viewed in other than the simplest and most tentative terms on the evidence of the confined excavation at Mills Mount, the use of that area as a rubbish tip may imply a smaller settlement than in the Iron Age, perhaps with its focus now confined to the summit. The change seems to be happening from the late fourth century, when a new kind of evidence begins to bear on the matter, consisting of lists of kings of the Gododdin, encountered at an earlier date as the Votadini. The whole subject is indistinct in the extreme, but kings of the Gododdin may from the end of the fourth century have resided on the Rock. An unexpected if rather ambiguous link between the Gododdin, their kings and the Rock, however, comes some two hundred years later from a new source which by one interpretation helps to bring together the story so far. Yet it must continually be stressed that we are moving among shadows. 'The Dark Ages' is now considered an old-fashioned term by historians and archaeologists to describe the period from the end of the fourth century. It is still highly appropriate for our subject, however, as we leave obscure Roman contacts in the past for an even more indistinct future.

Shadows

Before the 1988–91 excavations mentioned above, the earliest record of human activity that was reckoned to have taken place on the Rock was in literature, in an Old Welsh manuscript now preserved at Cardiff. The heroic elegy Y *Gododdin* was composed by the bard Aneirin in about AD 600:

The princely war-band of the king, called by the bard Mynyddog Mwynfawr, is gathered at Din Eidyn, the hill or stronghold of Eidyn (the 'Edin-' of *Edinburgh* is the same word as 'Eidyn'). Most have come there from the territories of the Gododdin ruled by the King, territories stretching from the Forth to the Tees. There are also some from beyond the Forth, and from the kingdom of Strathclyde, and from as far away as North Wales. In the taper-lit hall of the stronghold, with a fire of pine-logs continually burning, these three hundred men – or in another of the several texts of the poem, three hundred and sixty – pledge themselves in mead, wine and beer, according to ancient custom, to die in the service of their lord. They are described as wearing robes of purple and gold, with gold brooches and neck-bands or torcs, drinking from goblets of gold or silver or vessels of glass. Their arms stand ready – spears with ash or holly shafts, swords and a conspicuous shield ornamented with gold are mentioned. Soon, equipped with this weaponry, all but one (or three, together with the poet himself, according to the alternative version) of the band of cavalry are to die in a raid to the south into the lands of the Angles, at Catraeth (Catterick in Yorkshire) (6).

Aneirin sang of the year-long feasting and the heroic virtues of the doomed men in a heightened style of epic language and within a recognized poetic convention. He is not composing political or military history, and his elegy gives us only a tantalizing glimpse from the past. We cannot know with any certainty that the hall where the aristocracy of the Gododdin drank and feasted was near the summit of the Rock, for all the historical dimensions of Aneirin's masterpiece – save for the martial society he describes, which we know from many sources was true enough –

are subjects for debate. The king may have been only a figment, an exemplary hero. An eminent authority on the period argues that in any event the most attractive location for the hall of Eidyn is on an eminence below Arthur's Seat, where there is an archaeological site which, from its characteristics, may have been occupied around AD 600. It seems, however, to others, including the author, that the balance of probability is in favour of the Rock, and that other aspects of the poem are a useful source, though one to be used cautiously. Certainly our broad understanding of the time derived from archaeology suggests that, as might be expected, the poem embroiders reality: the heroes would not flaunt so much gold and they probably drank out of vessels of horn or wood, maybe with silver mounts. And our only specific archaeological insight into the Rock at this time is the existence of the large rat-infested rubbish tip below the citadel and about 100m (330ft) to the north-west of the most likely position of the hall of Eidyn.

The hall emerges as something exceptionally grand from Aneirin's passing references to it – a place of renown, sumptuous and most firmly constructed. Archaeological findings from elsewhere, together with documentary mentions and illustrations of other great buildings (7), suggest that it would have been constructed of timber – most likely with a timber frame infilled with clay, a steeply-pitched roof of shingles and several windows and doors. The timbers of the structure would have been ornamentally carved and the gable ends would have risen above the level of the roof ridge, with decorative terminals. The hall may have been a simple rectangle, like the largest building, measuring 28 by 9m (92 by 30ft), at the Anglian settlement at Sprouston (known from aerial photography), south of the Tweed near Kelso, which may be near contemporary. The site would have been fortified, though while the Iron Age settlement that preceded it may have given some basis for the defences, Din Eidyn's effective perimeter would perhaps have been restricted to the citadel, with walls of drystone, stone and turf, or a variation of these reinforced with timber framing. From such a hall on the Rock around AD 600, the real figure, presented to posterity by Aneirin as Mynyddog Mwynfawr, may have ruled. At around that date, the lists of the kings of the Gododdin give the name of Morgan Bulc.

With further Anglian advances the name of the kingdom and people of the Gododdin disappears from the north, though its traditions, with some of its people, emerge again in Wales. A place called *Etin* – a variant of (Din) Eidyn – was besieged in 638, and the reference has been taken to give the date when the Rock with its fortress changed owners to join the territories of the Angles, to become part of Northumbria. While the date may not be absolutely certain, the

7 *The Hall of Eidyn may have shared some of the characteristics of the Temple of Jerusalem as magnificently shown on the first page of St Luke's Gospel in the* Book of Kells *in Trinity College Dublin. This is admittedly an idealized sumptuous building of the period. The drawing shows 'the Temple' as a simple line drawing divorced from the figures that surround it on the original folio. Note the elaborate animal forms terminating the carved timbers of the roof, and the ornamentally shaped shingles forming the roof covering which may have been painted in different colours. As additional ornament, the walls are also covered in painted shingles.*

event is, and with the change of owners the language of the Rock also changed. The Old Welsh of the Gododdin was replaced by the northern strain of Anglo-Saxon spoken by the new occupants – a language which, through all later shifts of people and power, was to develop into Old Scots.

Both the Gododdin and the Angles were in these times Christians, but no one knows when a church was first built on the Rock. It has been suggested that the place of worship near the summit called in later records St Mary's Church originated as a Northumbrian foundation of the seventh century. There is a statement in the *Life of St Monenna*, of around AD 600, that the saint founded churches at a number of important places in the north including Edinburgh – not the most reliable authority, but as indicating some kind of tradition perhaps worth mentioning in passing. The site of St Mary's, whenever it was founded, must have seen more rebuildings and changes of function in its long history than perhaps any other in Scotland. It is now occupied by the Scottish National War Memorial.

No archaeological remains of these centuries on the Rock were found in the excavations of the

8 *A double-sided bone (possibly antler) comb found in the course of the Mills Mount excavation. Most probably of the seventh or eighth century* AD, *it may be either Pictish or Anglian. (Drawing by Marion O'Neil.)*

late 1980s, although a bone comb that might be either Anglian or Pictish was recovered (8). In view of the history that has been summarized above, an Anglian object would not be out of place, though Pictish associations may at first sight be unexpected. If Pictish, however, the comb would not stand alone, for not long after the creation of Princes Street Gardens in the 1820s a sculptured stone was found reused as a cover to a little bridge on one of the garden footpaths immediately below the Castle (9). It bore two of the enigmatic symbols of the Picts, a crescent and V-shaped rod and a double disc and Z-shaped rod. Though now lost, it was clearly of a type ascribed to the seventh century. We have seen that the permanent territories of the Picts lay mainly in eastern Scotland north of the Forth; in the late seventh century they were under heavy pressure from advancing Angles until the Picts routed them at Nechtanesmere (near Forfar in Angus) in 685. If the stone is evidence to be relied on – that of the comb is ambiguous – it might suggest a short Pictish occupation unrecorded by history, but just possible after that decisive battle. Whatever the truth of this may be, Northumbria subsequently consolidated her hold and her language in Lothian. We have no specific knowledge about the Rock at this time. It was presumably a fortified site of some importance, though the chief place of Northumbria remained at Bamburgh, on the coast of present-day Northumberland.

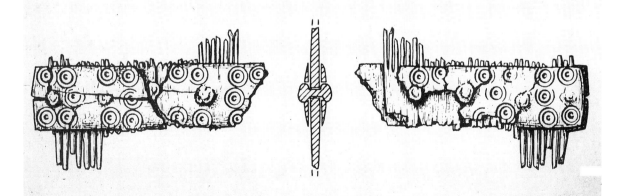

9 *Pictish stone with the crescent and V-shaped rod and (partly defaced) the double disc and Z-shaped rod, two of the unique series of symbols used by the Picts, found below the Castle Rock in the first part of the nineteenth century.*

A unified Scotland beyond the Forth was created about 844 when Pictland was joined to the kingdom of the Scots. A unified England did not emerge until the following century, when Scotland seems already to have begun to contest the possession of Lothian. Territory as far south as the Tweed finally passed into Scottish hands with Malcolm II's victory at the battle of Carham in 1018. The descendants of the Gaelic-speaking invaders from Ireland now ruled a state of very mixed origins in terms of language and culture, in which the old Anglian element with its stronghold at Edinburgh (we may now use the modern name without anachronism) was to rise to predominance.

CHAPTER TWO

Saint Margaret to Mons Meg

The king's castle

Malcolm III, son of Duncan, succeeded to the Scottish throne after the slaying of Macbeth in 1057. In about 1071, after the conquest of England by William of Normandy, Malcolm wedded Margaret, of the old Saxon royal house. Malcolm kept up hostilities against the new line of kings of England until he was killed at Alnwick in Northumberland in November 1093. On 16 November Queen Margaret, seriously ill in Edinburgh Castle, returned to her chamber from Mass to be met by her fourth son Edgar, who told her that her husband and eldest son had been slain in battle. The news caused her death, and it also prompted Malcolm's brother Donald Ban (the Donalbain of Shakespeare's *Macbeth*) to lay siege to the stronghold in a successful bid to seize the vacant throne. According to a narrative of the event Donald had by an odd oversight disregarded the western entry to the castle – it no longer exists, but was an easy ascent – and confined his blockade to the principal eastern approach. The Queen's body was taken by Prince Edgar through the west postern gate unobserved, and was buried in Dunfermline.

No evidence of buildings survives from this time, but the account of Margaret's death taken together with the topography of the Rock suggests the grouping of the royal lodgings and the hall adjacent to it near the church, within an inner fortification of the citadel-summit, a pattern that was broadly to last for several centur-ies. From this point onward, until the replanning completed just after 1500 created the great southern courtyard known today as Crown Square, the narrative will assume that the royal centre stood on the citadel-summit. In that centre the Queen, as we have noted, had her own private chamber, and King Malcolm would have had a separate chamber, to sleep, eat and receive in. Through the sometimes confusing develop-ment that leads up to what we would recognize as a royal palace in Edinburgh Castle we shall find the king and the queen with their own separate accommodation. In the eleventh century the Hall continues in its high importance for more public royal occasions, much as in the time of the Gododdin, and (on the interpretation we have followed) it must have stood on or near the site of the hall of Eidyn.

Although Malcolm III had continually fought William I and William Rufus of England, his court, with one of its chief centres at Edinburgh Castle, increasingly adopted Anglo-Norman customs and culture. It was in the reign of Malcolm and Margaret that the decisive steps were taken that began to erode the ancient social fabric of the Scottish kingdom, to introduce what was to be called the 'feudal system' of relationships in duty, backed up by law, between the king and the pyramid of peer groups beneath him, and to give a new focus to our subject: the stronghold on the Rock had become a feudal castle.

A period of strife, with four kings in as many

years, followed Malcolm III's death. Then from 1097 to 1153 the surviving sons of Malcolm and Margaret ruled Scotland in succession as King Edgar, Alexander I and David I. The functions of the king's castles throughout the realm now began to emerge. A simplified image of medieval castles sees them as more or less heavily fortified versions of the stately homes of more recent times; and although this may be true up to a point, the reality was more complicated, especially for royal castles. They were certainly defensible and some like Edinburgh were of great and, as time went on, increasing strength. Of equal importance, they certainly provided a dwelling for royalty and the royal household, though no castle, not even the most important, was a permanent residence, for the household constantly travelled from one place to another. The movement was caused not only for reasons of state or change of scene but also because of housekeeping necessity. Most of the dues from the king's personal domain were payable in kind, including foodstuffs. After a limited stay, new provisions were found by moving somewhere else. Besides, rudimentary or non-existent sanitation meant that any house soon became unpleasantly dirty, which gave another good reason for a literally fresh start.

The king did not live only at his own castles. Important subjects might receive him, and with the royal foundation of monasteries he could establish himself in the guest-house. Indeed at monasteries such as Dunfermline (founded about 1068 by Queen Margaret) and Holyrood (by her son David I in 1128) it is arguable that the guest-houses were built with a very limited range of guests chiefly in mind – the king or his consort. From the beginning these were embryonic palaces, whose amenity and status as palaces was in time to overtake that of the royal castles.

To receive payment in kind, a royal castle such as Edinburgh had also to be a storehouse, and it was the centre for the management of the surrounding royal lands. It was the headquarters of the Sheriff, who was also the Keeper of the Castle. The Sheriff was the administrative officer for his sheriffdom or shire on behalf of the king, and he held a court of justice in the castle as the centre of his jurisdiction. The Sheriff and the higher judges, or justiciars, of the kingdom levied fines, which were among the earliest money resources available to the Crown. The Sheriff also maintained a prison in the king's castle for the administration of justice, and this was to be one of the most enduring functions of Edinburgh Castle. It was used alike as a State prison for great offences such as treason, and as a common jail.

Edinburgh was one of a few royal castles which emerged with an especial prominence, one reason being perhaps its key place in the wealthy and influential ex-Northumbrian part of the realm. At some time between 1139 and 1150 David I held an Assembly in the Castle, with churchmen, earls and barons summoned to attend. It is the first identified location for a meeting of the body that was to evolve into the Parliament of Scotland.

David I, either as Earl of Cumbria (then part of Scotland) before his accession to the throne, or more likely as king from 1124 until 1153, was almost certainly responsible for the oldest surviving building on the Castle Rock. It has been long known as St Margaret's Chapel (10) after David's mother, who was canonized as St Margaret in 1250. David may indeed have built it as a royal chapel to commemorate his mother. The chapel would in this private capacity supplement St Mary's Church close by to the south, where David I, with his passion to advance the ecclesiastical establishment, also ordained substantial work to be done. As visible today, the structural history of the chapel is obscure because of the drastic alterations that

10 *The exterior of St Margaret's Chapel, most probably built by Margaret's son David I in the 1130s or 1140s. The building was much altered for military use as a magazine and store from the sixteenth to the nineteenth centuries. It was restored in 1851–2, and the doorway was remodelled to its present form in 1939.*

were later to be made to it, not least its conversion to a magazine when the Castle functioned as a major Scottish arsenal.

It has been suggested that the chapel was part of something larger, perhaps even the royal lodgings, and certainly there is an apparent incongruity between the simple oblong of the exterior and the quite sophisticated plan inside (**11**). The interior is divided into two compartments, a rectangular nave and a sanctuary in the form of a rounded apse with a half-dome. The two are separated by a Romanesque arch, jambs with nook-shafts or small columns (renewed during restoration in 1851–2), the arch itself being enriched with a chevron pattern (**12**). Although the half-dome of the apse is original, the barrel-vault over the nave was added during the use of the chapel as a magazine. Within the apse is a north doorway and an aumbry or cupboard for the vessels of the Sacrament.

It is impossible to fix on an exact date of building for the chapel. When it was rediscovered in the middle of the nineteenth century, it was thought to be the same building where Margaret had worshipped. No architectural historian would now accept that it could be so early because of the detail of the chancel arch,

and the earliest possible date recently proposed is around 1110. It has however been pointed out that close analogies with detail at Holyrood and Dunfermline suggest, more conservatively, the 1130s or 1140s.

The royal importance of Edinburgh Castle is increasingly underlined at this period. David I's elder brother Edgar had often lived in the Castle and he died there. It was one of four places where David stayed most frequently (the others being Stirling Castle and the monasteries of Scone and Dunfermline). His grandson and successor, Malcolm IV, apparently resided in Edinburgh Castle more than anywhere else during his reign from 1153 to 1165. In addition to its use by royalty, by the end of the century new functions appear to have been given to the place. After he was captured at Alnwick during an invasion of England in 1174, William the Lion was obliged to admit English garrisons to the castles of Berwick upon Tweed, Edinburgh, Jedburgh, Roxburgh and Stirling as one of the conditions

11 *St Margaret's Chapel: plan drawn by Sir Henry Dryden showing the blocked openings as found by Daniel Wilson in 1846.*

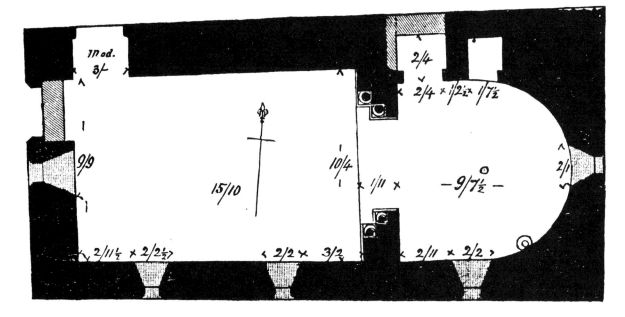

12 *St Margaret's Chapel: the chancel arch.*

for his release. Edinburgh Castle was not recovered until 1186 and when the English king's garrison withdrew, the Records of Scotland seem to have been lodged there, beginning an association with the national archives which was to last until 1692. It is possible that the Scottish Treasury and the Crown Jewels also had a permanent home there from the 1190s.

Outside the Castle, Edinburgh had been created a royal burgh at the beginning of the reign of David I. While Edinburgh was soon politically eminent, partly because of its history and location, it was not the most substantial burgh, for Berwick upon Tweed was a good deal more prosperous. Several centuries elapsed before Edinburgh may be called the capital of Scotland in the sense of a permanent location of national government. Indeed, what there was of continuous national government (for much responsibility was devolved to the landowners, the Church and the burghs) moved about the country with the king and his household. The royal household contained within itself much of the limited administrative apparatus of state.

The fight for Scotland

The royal castles as they survive today retain few early features. Yet during the thirteenth century, to the end of the reign of Alexander III (1249–86), Edinburgh Castle may have shared in that development of military architecture which produced advanced baronial castles like Bothwell, Caerlaverock or Kildrummy, with their high towers and massive curtain walls. Relying on the natural features of the site, Edinburgh's perimeter may not have had such sophisticated defences, but its upper ward probably had a complement of encircling towers. This is a surmise based on likelihood and a later rather fanciful drawing, for there are no sure masonry remains of the thirteenth-century defences, and absolutely nothing of domestic buildings of that date; although the excavations of 1988–91 set down some new fragments of knowledge on to a fairly blank sheet. The western approach was protected by double ditches of large scale, which may possibly have had a prehistoric origin. There was a substantial road at Mills Mount leading towards the west postern: the excavators have commented that while a romantic imagination may see it as the road along which Queen Margaret's bier was taken from the Castle in 1093, its archaeological context more prosaically

13 *St Margaret's Chapel, probably built between 1130 and 1150 (1) highlighted on a drawing of the late twentieth-century Castle. St Mary's Church was sited where the Scottish National War Memorial (2) now stands. Here on the summit, shown enclosed by an oval line, would be grouped the other chief buildings, in particular the Hall and the Royal Lodgings. (The outline view of the Castle here and in later drawings was prepared by Heather Insh.)*

puts its likely beginnings in the thirteenth century (**14**). In this area, too, there were traces of a smithy, which after a more solid rebuilding was to go on in use for a long time.

When Alexander III's young queen wrote to her father, Henry III of England, she described the site rather than its accommodation – this 'sad and solitary place, without greenery and, because of its nearness to the sea, unwholesome' (a comment on the thick sea-mist or haar which still only too often envelops the Castle). Her private lodging is named in 1278 as 'St Margaret's Chamber'. The name may imply the survival of the room on the summit where the now canonized queen of Malcolm III had died nearly two hundred years before – though perhaps it had been 'modernized' in the interval. Alternatively, it may refer to a scheme of decoration having as its subject the life of Scotland's royal saint.

With the disputed succession to the kingdom after the deaths of Alexander III in 1286, and his grand-daughter the Maid of Norway four years later, Alexander's brother-in-law and friend, Edward I of England, son of Henry III, undertook to adjudicate between the rival claimants. During the proceedings Edward, with his pretended authority as feudal superior and lord paramount of Scotland – an authority which the Scots did not at this time seriously dispute – visited Edinburgh in the summer of 1291 to receive homage from the country's notables, an event which probably took place in the Castle. At the Scottish burgh of Berwick upon Tweed in November 1292 he determined the succession in favour of John Baliol. The new king did homage to Edward at the end of the year as the King of England's vassal; but Edward's overbearing conduct as superior soon alienated even King John, whose alliance with France and rebellion in 1295 led to personal humiliation and national disaster.

In the spring of 1296 Edward I invaded Scotland and besieged Edinburgh Castle at an early stage in the campaign of 21 weeks that temporarily extinguished Scottish independence.

14 *The medieval road leading to the west postern entry of the Castle, found during the archaeological excavations of 1988–91 at Mills Mount. It is most likely to belong to the thirteenth century.*

Edward's throwing-engines – giant catapults like the ballistae of Roman times – hurled stones through the roofs of the buildings within the walls continually for three days and nights before the place surrendered (**15–16**). The muniments, relics and treasure in the Castle were sent to England. A list of the 'jewels found in Edinburgh Castle' sent to London with John le Candelar included a shrine with the King of Scotland's arms, crystal goblets mounted in silver-gilt, ivory horns decorated with silk and silver, with many silver cups, basins and silver-mounted wooden drinking bowls. Edinburgh Castle now held a garrison for Edward as opposition to his claimed authority increased. Its numbers varied: in 1300 there were 347 persons in the place – knights and their attendants,

soldiers, priests, clerks and household servants, with 156 horses. In 1302 the numbers had been reduced to 81 men, but it is not clear whether such fluctuations were a response to a changing degree of threat or simply reflect the administrative difficulty of keeping distant bodies of men at a stable level.

The degree of threat was, however, to change within a few years. Robert 'the Bruce', crowned at Scone in March 1306 as King Robert I, was able to provide powerful new leadership for the Scots (18) while the death of the implacable Edward I in the following year brought his ineffective son to the throne of England. In the next years the Scots took the initiative, and among other events a surprise attack by Thomas Randolph, Earl of Moray, nephew of King Robert, recaptured Edinburgh Castle in 1314 from Edward II's Sheriff of Edinburgh, a Gascon knight called Peres Lebaud. The Earl of Moray's plan seems spectacularly dangerous, for the advance party of thirty which, under William Francis, made the difficult ascent of a rudimentary alpine track up the north precipice, scaled the wall on top and, taking the garrison by surprise, admitted reinforcements by the main gates and won the place. The Scottish king ordered the dismantling of the defences to prevent reoccupation by his adversaries. Within the castle, nothing is recorded as being actively preserved except St Margaret's Chapel, which

17 *A silver penny of Edward II found in the course of archaeological excavations at Edinburgh Castle. The coin is the only recognizable memento of its capture and occupation by Edward's father, the 'Hammer of the Scots'. Edward II lost the Castle in 1314, the year of Bannockburn.*

was being repaired in 1329, the year of Robert I's death. In passing we may note another variant in the language of the Rock. We have encountered first British or Old Welsh, then northern Anglo-Saxon beginning to mutate into Old Scots. Now, in the higher social stratum at least, we find French – not just from the lips of native-born Frenchmen like Lebaud, but from Scots and Englishmen too.

In 1314 the future of an independent Scotland was for a time secured by Bannockburn; much later, Bruce's sword was being reverently kept in a strong vault of Edinburgh Castle. The threat from England, however, was renewed within two decades. From 1333 Edward III repeated his grandfather's endeavour to rule over Scotland as a vassal kingdom. Again he had much support from Scots, for opinion on the English connection was and remained divided, and he was able to put Edward Baliol, son of King John, on the throne. The dismantled Edinburgh Castle was occupied in 1335 by a detachment of Edward's army under Guy, Count of Namur. The count was then forced to surrender after a day and a night, but in the same year the place was again garrisoned by the English, who carried out considerable repairs to the defences as well

15 (Above left) *A replica of a medieval catapult, which might be used in a siege either by the attack or the defence. The arm containing a stone projectile is pulled back, twisting ropes at the base of the arm. The arm when released springs forward and throws the stone. This example is at Caerlaverock Castle, Dumfriesshire.*

16 (Below left) *The largest type of throwing-engine called a trébuchet, shown as an illumination on a charter of the city of Carlisle dated 1316. A trébuchet was operated by a counterpoised weight rather than by twisted ropes. The heavily weighted and tapered beam, when released, swung to throw a missile placed in the opposite end of the beam.*

as – again – to St Margaret's Chapel, the Great Chamber and the stable.

The Great Chamber is another part of the king's personal accommodation. It is not known when it was built, but it would have been provided in addition to the king's private chamber or Lodging which, with the Queen's Chamber, has already been remarked on; and like these, the Great Chamber would be part of the group on the summit. Later in the Middle Ages a Great Chamber performed some of the functions of the private lodging, but in a more public fashion and with more formality. It was a place for audience and for dining on a fairly large scale – the largest occasions would be placed in the Hall – in general a room of ceremony, and a location where business of state might be carried on. In England the Great Chamber was to become entirely a place of affairs. It was also used by those close to the monarch without the royal presence. Why the servants of the English king repaired this room in Edinburgh Castle we do not know, but it is an intriguing possibility that the work might have been done in anticipation of a visit to Scotland by Edward III, which in the event was not to happen.

With this programme of work in hand within the Castle, in 1336 Sir Andrew Moray of Bothwell, Guardian of Scotland in the minority of Bruce's son David II, unsuccessfully besieged it, and a little later the English Warden Sir Thomas de Rokeby is found trying to secure the position of himself and the garrison by continuing repairs, including a new gate. These precautions proved irrelevant in the recapture of the place by a storybook stratagem on 17 April 1341, devised by William of Douglas and others. Disguised as merchants and their servants bring-

18 *Statue of King Robert I (Robert the Bruce) in a niche added to the façade of the Victorian gatehouse of Edinburgh Castle, made in 1929 by the sculptor Thomas Clapperton to commemorate the 600th anniversary of the King's death. The niche was designed by Robert Lorimer.*

ing supplies to the garrison – 49 men-at-arms, 60 mounted archers and 6 watchmen – a party contrived to drop its loads so as to prevent the closing of the gates. Joined by the main force concealed nearby, they overcame resistance. On taking the castle Douglas and his companions disposed of most of their opponents by cutting their throats or decapitating them, and throwing the bodies over the crags.

Scotland now seemed safe enough for the return of the seventeen-year-old David II, who had spent his childhood and adolescence in France. The young king landed in his realm on 2 June 1341. Edinburgh Castle was strengthened with defensive stone-throwing machines in 1342, while the young king began a sustained offensive against Edward III's garrisons, which in a few years left only Berwick upon Tweed in English hands. Edward was now distracted from his claim to the overlordship of Scotland in a way that his grandfather had never been. As Duke of Aquitaine he became increasingly and successfully involved in French affairs, assuming the title of King of France in 1340. David II was taking advantage of this major distraction and playing his part in the Franco-Scottish alliance initiated half a century earlier by King John Baliol. His role came to an abrupt end in 1346 with an expedition into England to try to relieve pressure on his ally. Both parties to the alliance suffered disaster; France most conspicuously in a crushing defeat at Crécy; while in an engagement at Neville's Cross with Edward III's lieutenants, the King of Scots, wounded in the face, was captured. He was not released from imprisonment, spent mostly in the Tower of London, until 1356, on promise to pay a ransom by instalments.

On his return David proceeded with improvements to Edinburgh Castle, possibly using some of the funds raised for the payment of the ransom. His first enterprise seems to have been a reconstruction, complete by 1366, of St Mary's Church, which had been altered for use as a granary during the last English occupation. A better water-supply was provided, and in 1362

Roger Hog, a burgess of Edinburgh high in the king's favour, built the Well-House Tower at a well below the north precipice. The tower survives today as a not-very-comprehensible ruin. Its main function was not to defend the well, but to protect the starting-off point for the precipitous ascent of the north face of the Rock, by which the Castle had been surprised in 1314 by William Francis's daring party. This route seems now to have been improved to make it a rather more feasible – though still hazardous – communication.

The king then turned his attention to the main perimeter of the place. In 1367–8 a massive L-shaped tower was begun on top of the eastern crags, above the grassy ridge of the Castle Hill. The tower, later named David's Tower (the first time it was so called was in 1448), was intended as a new private royal lodging as well as the most formidable element of the defences towards the burgh (**19**). Its ruin survives – the tower was shattered by siege in 1573, and what is left is not visible from any external viewpoint because the Half-Moon Battery is now wrapped round it – and gives several clues to the planning of its main accommodation. The lowest level is a vault that may have served as a strongroom of the Scottish Treasury. Above is the King's Lodging consisting of a private hall below a chamber; and probably superimposed on that was a new Queen's Lodging: an early, large and (with its two lodgings) relatively sophisticated example of what was to see many variants as a 'tower-house' plan in Scotland.

Where the ideas behind its design came from is hard to say, but David had had plenty of opportunity to see some of the best of international castle design during his refuge in France and imprisonment in England. David's Tower is not only important in its own regard, but its construction marks the abandonment of the King's old Lodging on the summit.

From the Age of Chivalry

David II died in the Castle in February 1371. The tower he had begun as a strongpoint and personal lodging was completed during the reign of his successor, Robert II (1371–90), the first of the long line of the Stewarts (or Stuarts, as the name of the monarch was spelt from the time of Mary Queen of Scots). Soon David's Tower was extended to make its original L-shaped plan a rectangle, and further projects were put in hand. A new main north-eastern gate-tower seems now

to have been built, to be called the Constable's Tower as the residence of the Constable or Keeper. It was given a yett, or grille-like iron gate, in 1377, and was finished with paving and a drawbridge in 1383. By then the Hall up on the summit had been re-roofed, a kitchen and other service buildings had been raised beside David's Tower, and a stone kennel had been erected for the royal dogs. Significantly in view of later developments, in Robert II's reign a small armaments industry was growing up in the Castle. Bows, crossbows and throwing-engines were being made there, the manufacture of the throwing-engines being the special responsibility of a carpenter called Dedric, who may have either been Flemish or German (Dietrich).

19 *David's Tower, at the top of this drawing of 1544 dominating the east front of the Castle.*

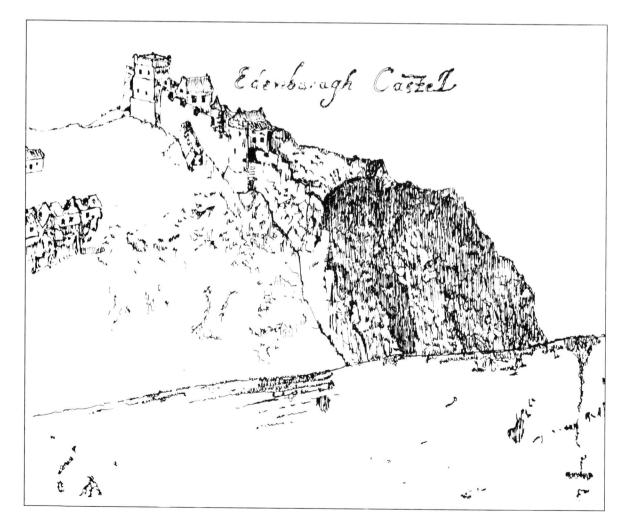

The fourteenth century was the period of the invention and early development of firearms in Europe. Alongside the traditional weapons that have just been noted, 'an instrument called a gun' was bought for the Castle at a cost of £4 in 1384, with sulphur and saltpetre for making gunpowder. The modest purchase is a token of the new age for warfare in general, as it is for our immediate subject; and while it is not known when the Castle's smiths began to make guns themselves on the premises, they already had the skills to produce at least the smaller types of wrought and forged iron artillery. The location of the smithy where weapons were made is not known. The 1988–91 excavations showed that around this time the smithy at Mills Mount was very active, but there was no sign that it made implements of war.

The stronghold's artillery may soon have been tested in action against the Auld Enemy, for although the Castle was not besieged in Richard II's advance to Edinburgh in 1385, it held out against Henry V in 1400. Henry's expedition to Scotland was made with the object of receiving the homage of Robert III, which Robert refused to give. The kings of England had not given up their claim to be overlords of Scotland. But the claim had lost the ferocious drive brought to it by Edward I and, at least in the early years of his reign, by Edward III. In no small part this relaxation was due to the continuing distraction of affairs in France, and there was also in progress some increase in Scotland's relative strength; whatever the reason, it was a contrast with the recent past.

Henry V in 1400 was said to have held back from whole-heartedly devastating the countryside out of a chivalrous respect for Robert III's Queen Annabella. The supposition is unlikely, though the magnanimous code of gallantry, honour and courtesy did very occasionally trespass into politics. We are, after all, in the flood tide of chivalry, the ideal of the knight without fear and without reproach. The Frenchman Jean Froissart, whose writings are reckoned to be infused with the high principles of knighthood, had visited the Scottish court, but was impressed neither by Edinburgh which 'notwithstanding it is the residence of the King, and is the Paris of Scotland, is not such a town as Tournai or Valenciennes; for there are not in the whole town four hundred houses', nor by the Scots nobility and gentry, recording his view that 'in Scotland you will never find a man of worth; they are like savages ... ignorant hypocrites and traitors'. Whatever their alleged moral shortcomings the Scots certainly went through the motions of chivalrous exercise. Tournaments were staged at the lists or tilting ground near the King's Stables, just below the south side of the Rock where the place-name, though not any visible evidence of building, survives. David II and Edward III of England had shared the spirit of the age, with David enjoying tournaments at the English court as well as in Scotland. At one of these knightly war games held under the Castle Rock at Edinburgh in 1398 and graced by Queen Annabella, her eldest son, the recently created Duke of Rothesay took part.

Robert III's reign ended in 1406 when the ailing king died on hearing that his second son, now his heir (the Duke of Rothesay had recently died under mysterious circumstances) had been captured by the English while voyaging to France. This son succeeded as James I but remained in captivity until 1424. For much of the time authority rested with his uncle, the Duke of Albany. During Albany's administration, as indeed in earlier governments, office-bearers helped themselves to the revenue from the customs as a self-awarded fee. Two would-be beneficiaries, the Earl of Douglas and Sir William Crawford, fell out over the expected spoils at some time between 1416 and 1418, and Douglas besieged Crawford in Edinburgh Castle as a simple way to settle their difference of opinion.

The return of James I to Scotland, like that of David II, involved the payment of a ransom, claimed as 'expenses' for his long enforced stay in England. The King then spent much of his reign from 1424 until 1437 in Edinburgh Castle.

Again James I, like David II, used the obligation to pay the ransom as a means of increasing the general financial resources of the Crown, including those directed towards building projects. Considerable sums were spent on improvements in the Castle from 1433. In that year there was work on the walls, and a beginning was made on the construction of a new Great Chamber for the King above extensive vaults, possibly part of the kitchen and service cellars located next to the 'great tower' and paid for in 1382. The work was completed and paid for only in 1445. The vaults survive, together with a considerable structure – the nucleus of the present Palace – that is very hard to interpret in terms of its building history because of later changes. What appears to have emerged was a rectangular block with its east side enclosing the Great Chamber which rose to the full height of the building, its windows above the south-eastern crags opening to superb prospects of town and country (after intermediate changes, the Great Chamber was altered and subdivided in the seventeenth century into what are now called the 'King's Dining Room' and its anteroom, and its roof was lowered). The west side of the block was clearly less important, containing smaller rooms, probably lodgings, on two or three floors. Such a 'double-pile' building – two ranges joined together side by side – would be extraordinarily precocious in the fifteenth century, and James I's contribution may have been less than the complete rectangular edifice.

The construction of the new Great Chamber, with the king's private lodging still incorporating his private hall in David's Tower, continues the theme of royal accommodation in the Castle; while the rectangular block initiated by James I, however the time-scale of its construction is interpreted, must be seen as a hinge in the overall development of the interior of the Castle. With his contribution, James made a first move towards the major southern courtyard, today's 'Crown Square', to which the royal centre was to be transferred.

On a different aspect of castle planning, the year 1433 also saw the establishment of a royal herb garden. This pleasure garden – the medieval 'herb garden' was meant to be walked about in and enjoyed – reminds us that even a massive stronghold like Edinburgh Castle offered something of *la douceur de la vie* to its well-born residents, such as James's eldest son and the Keeper, Sir William Crichton, who was also according to custom Sheriff of Edinburgh. Both had a lodging in the Castle, and repairs were carried out to their kitchens at this time.

The King was murdered in 1437 and the son just mentioned succeeded as James II (20). Crichton retained his offices and became Chancellor – the highest Scottish office of state – in 1439. He was later remembered as 'a man of great foresight and singular manhood, and a faithful subject and sure shield of the common good'. Crichton took James II into his care, or perhaps rather custody, in the Castle, and exploited this advantageous position in a spectacular political assassination to check the excessive power of the Douglases. On 24 November 1440 Crichton, with the child king, received the sixth Earl of Douglas and his brother at the Castle 'with great joy and gladness', and 'banqueted royally with all delicacies that could be got. After great cheer was made at the dinner and courses taken away' Crichton 'presented a bull's head before the earl which was a sign and token of condemnation to death'. In spite of the king's protestations at such an outrage of hospitality the Douglases were taken from the table, given summary trial and beheaded for alleged treason.

Edinburgh Castle, toun [dwellings, lodgings] and
    tower,
God grant thou sink for sin
And that even for the black dinner
Earl Douglas got therein.

The Castle did not sink, however; nor in the longer term did Crichton. The next-but-one successor to the Douglas title, William eighth Earl, warily reinforced his family's position and

20 *James II (1437–60): a portrait in the Württemberg State Library.*

Jacob von gots
genaden küng
von Schottland

out-schemed Crichton, who lost favour and was deprived of his offices late in 1444. In the following year James II besieged the former Chancellor in Edinburgh Castle and after a nine weeks' siege the place surrendered, though on terms favourable to Crichton. Repairs followed from 1447 to 1449: to the king's kitchen, to David's Tower and the gate-tower – all these may have been a consequence of siege damage. Meanwhile Crichton had proved himself still so

21 *Mons Meg with iron and stone shot.*

influential that he was reconciled to the king, created Lord Crichton and reappointed Chancellor, a post which he held until his death in 1454. By then in an unplanned repeat performance of the Black Dinner, the king himself had killed the eighth Earl of Douglas in a quarrel after supper at Stirling Castle.

In spite of a superficial appearance of turmoil, the economic strength of Scotland, based on the growing burghs and the money resources of her rulers, had increased significantly from the time of David II to James II. The improvement had been reflected in the chief royal castles, both in new buildings and in new weapons, for the first recorded Scottish gun of 1384 was followed by others including the giant siege pieces called bombards. When James II began to demonstrate his personal rule from 1453 with domestic campaigns against over-mighty subjects including the Douglases, his artillery carried out a series of successful sieges.

In 1457 James was given one of the most famous of guns. The great bombard or siege piece now called Mons Meg was manufactured to the order of Philip the Good, Duke of Burgundy, by his artillery maker Jehan Cambier (**21**). It was tested at Mons in 1449. In 1457

'Mons' was sent by the duke with a sister gun and artillery supplies as a present to James II of Scotland, whose queen was the duke's niece. Mons survives as a remarkable example of the heaviest type of artillery of its age. The barrel and the breech chamber are made from separate parts fixed together. The construction of the barrel, of 496mm (20in) calibre at the muzzle, is analogous to that of an ordinary wooden barrel;

22 *The location of buildings constructed up to 1460 which at least in part survive above ground in an identifiable form, highlighted on a drawing of the twentieth-century castle: St Margaret's Chapel (1); the ruin of David's Tower, begun in 1368, (2) with the Half-Moon wrapped round it; and the Great Chamber of 1433–45 (3) forming the core of the later Palace. It is noteworthy how very little is still in evidence close to the end of the Middle Ages.*

hence the name. Long wrought-iron bars were in effect welded together to form a cylinder over a core, and iron hoops were then shrunk over the bars. The massive breech chamber was hammer-forged from several masses of red-hot iron smelted in separate batches: no iron furnace of that date was large enough to produce so much metal at a single firing. The breech was then firmly locked on to the barrel, in a fashion that was only revealed when X-ray photographs were taken of the whole piece in the early 1980s. The built-up weapon, a remote ancestor of Sir William Armstrong's revolutionary armaments of the Victorian era, is a vivid reminder of the capability of medieval technology.

Mons, or Mons Meg as Philip's surviving bombard was later called (**colour plate 6**), was to have a long association with Edinburgh Castle. It was not kept there from the beginning, for when it arrived in Scotland no graded road existed in the Castle on which it could readily be taken inside the defences – and the guns of the siege train had to be easily transportable to and from their place of storage. A bombard (probably not Mons herself) brought to the Castle in 1459 for repair had to be left outside the gate and worked on there. The repair was part of the preparation for James II's move against Roxburgh Castle, the chief remaining English post in Scotland apart from Berwick upon Tweed. In the 1460 siege of Roxburgh the king was killed when one of his guns burst – James, 'more curious than became him or the majesty of a king', was indulging his fascination with artillery by standing close by as a salvo was fired to welcome his queen, who had come to visit the camp.

CHAPTER THREE

Summit of Prestige

Renaissance princes

The new gunpowder weapons required a more costly and elaborate military establishment than before, and it was to be increasingly concentrated in Edinburgh Castle. The first stage of a passable access road to take the heaviest siege pieces from the eastern approach to the summit – the first version of the route that exists today – seems to have been completed during the reign of James III (1460–88). In 1466 Gunner Dietrich, who may have been descended from the weapons-carpenter of the previous century, was maintaining the king's bombards and other artillery inside the Castle, the maintenance including painting the iron guns with red lead and protecting the timber of their mountings with pitch. Arrows, lances and other war material were still being made in the Castle workshops, and guns were probably being made there too. The increasing demands of the arsenal were to be met as a side-effect of the major internal replanning of the Castle which has already been mentioned, though the primary concern of the replanning was with the Castle as royal residence and centre for great affairs of State.

James III (23) had a special interest in Edinburgh for he passed most of his adult life in the Castle. Every Parliament of his reign, save one at Stirling, was held in Edinburgh. So far Parliaments and General Councils had been held in many places, depending on the location of the court, and 34 different places are recorded. Of these, Perth had seen most of the Parliaments, then Edinburgh, Scone and Stirling. In Edinburgh, Parliament still used the Castle. There, for example, the Hall had been made ready for a session of 1458 with new pieces of (waxed) linen cloth provided for the windows; glass was still rarely used save in churches. Parliament also, however, met in the Tolbooth, the all-purpose municipal building of every Scottish burgh, in the High Street by St Giles Church. The royal burghs had now over a long period been closely linked to the Crown, which placed considerable reliance on them for both financial and political support – the burghs providing in some measure a counter-balance to the often disruptive power of the great landowners – and the summons to Parliament of representatives of the royal burghs had become normal. Hence the frequent use of the burgh tolbooths, such as that of Stirling where Parliament had sat in 1439, and especially that of Edinburgh, where the Tolbooth, the 'Heart of Midlothian', was later to become the only place in the country where Parliament met. It seems reasonable to believe that James III's Edinburgh Parliaments were shared between castle and burgh, and with the settling of Parliament, Edinburgh finally emerged as the capital city (already hinted at in Froissart's reference to Edinburgh as the Paris of Scotland): it was James III who formally declared Edinburgh as the chief burgh of the kingdom.

The replanning of the Castle, providing it with a new principal courtyard, the quadrangle once

called Palace Yard and now Crown Square, was in the author's view completed by James IV (1488–1513) (**colour plate 7**), although the development of the concept and the progress of its construction have been a matter of debate, and from any standpoint are something of an enigma.

The contrivance of the courtyard was a mighty undertaking. First of all the whole of the site sloping from St Mary's Church to the brink of the southern precipices had to be raised to a uniform level on a labyrinthine series of vaults and sub-vaults; a series that had begun with the vaults under the 1433–45 Great Chamber. Only when this substructure had been created could major buildings be erected on the artificial platform above. In spite of its scale, the operation is hardly documented, and internal dating evidence, though most valuable, is sparse. In consequence, there is not much to say about the progress of the building campaign beyond the obvious remark that it seems too much to cram into the reign of James IV.

The previous monarch, James III, might seem a favoured candidate to have made a significant contribution, for one side of his character is described in terms that might delineate a prince of the Renaissance, preferring the company of literary men to that of his nobility, and delighting in the arts, especially music and architecture. Although it must be emphasized that recent historical opinion has painted a picture of James III as being as ineffective as a builder as he was ineffective in most other fields, it is still attractive to think that he helped to shape the new look of Edinburgh Castle.

Some of the vaults just mentioned were to be used during most of their existence for the obvious function of storage, and a few are still stores today. Some appear to have been associated with the arsenal. At least two sub-vaults

23 *James III (1460–88) spent much of his reign in the Castle, but although he was much interested in architecture it is a matter of debate how much he may have contributed to its development.*

were intended from the beginning as prisons, for the Castle was still the Sheriff's prison. Others, however, provided from the start most with fireplaces, may have been the earliest recognizable purpose-built accommodation for a garrison. At the time, the later part of the fifteenth century, a royal stronghold was warded at all times but was only 'stuffed with men' in times of crisis, for Scotland did not have a standing army, as we would understand the term, to provide garrisons until a long time afterwards. When such a regular army was formed, some vaults were used for the soldiers until the middle of the eighteenth century, when the accommodation – spreading to other vaults of the substructure – began to be used to confine prisoners taken in Britain's continental wars.

Turning to the buildings around the new courtyard, the west side above the vaults is the most likely site for the House of the Artillery recorded in 1498, later called the Gunhouse. This may seem an odd adjunct to a royal centre, but monarchs were extremely proud of their heavier weaponry, and the House of the Artillery may be seen as something of a showpiece. On the opposite side of the courtyard – making a contrast between war and peace – James IV seems to have made modifications and built, or at least finished, additions to the 1433–45 Great Chamber. Two fireplaces characteristic of about 1500 have generally been attributed to his reign (**24**). More open to discussion, however, is the dating of a southward extension providing a large Inner Chamber together with the Cabinet or small private room which later was to be famous as the birthplace of the prince who became James VI of Scotland and James I of England. Opening from the enlarged royal suite to the east were three fine oriel windows, commanding a magnificent view of burgh and countryside. The balance of likelihood is, in my view, that all of this enlargement and ornament was ordained by James IV (rather than being spread between his reign and the next).

The construction is an important step in the evolution of what we might recognize as a Royal

47

Palace in the Castle, and seems also to be significant in the more general story of palace planning. As far as we can tell there were still private Lodgings for both James IV and his queen (or future queen) in David's Tower. The Lodgings had a narrow and tortuous communication with the suite just created by James but were not an integral part of it. The new suite was more spacious, and probably more splendid, than the Lodgings, and may be seen as a very early example of a sequence of grand Rooms of State. Such an interpretation seems to be buttressed by the fact that it was here, and not in the Queen's Lodging, that James's grand-daughter Mary Queen of Scots resided when she came to the Castle before and at the time of the birth of her child – a grand event of the greatest national importance.

The date of the Great Hall, the building on the south side of the courtyard, is also a source of debate for architectural historians. The author's view is that around 1503 James IV completed a new hall here to replace the ancient structure on the summit of the Rock as the chief place of large-scale ceremony, banqueting and State assembly, including sessions of Parliament. It is not unlikely that the structure may have been already planned, and perhaps begun, even before James IV ascended the throne; but its completion should be linked, in my view, to James's marriage in 1503 to Henry VII's daughter Margaret Tudor, called by contemporaries the marriage of the Thistle and the Rose. The marriage of a King of Scots would always be considered an important event, and this one was seen as pre-eminently so, creating a peaceful link between two countries that for two centuries had been in a state of recurrent war. It is not therefore

24 *A fireplace which from its style belongs to the reign of James IV in the room now called 'The King's Dining Room' in the Palace of Edinburgh Castle, and conjecturally part of the Great Chamber begun by James I in 1433. The Great Chamber seems to have been subdivided in the seventeenth century to form this room.*

surprising that the match, once anticipated, would be commemorated by a substantial programme of building. The improvement of the Palace in the Castle has already been noted, and there was major and firmly documented work at Holyrood – not to mention places further afield in Scotland – for the occasion.

A date for the last stages of the Great Hall within James IV's reign is given by some of the carved stone corbels that bear the fine hammerbeam timber roof of the Hall. Two of the corbels have a thistle and a rose in a flower pot, while others have James's cipher 'IR4' – *Iacobus rex quartus* (**colour plate 8**). Yet these features, which seem to give such unambiguous evidence, have given rise to doubt because their Renaissance form would be extraordinarily precocious in Scotland at this time. They have the same classically-inspired idiom as the corbels of the great cornice of François I's building at the château of Blois, begun in 1515, one of the revolutionary buildings of western European architecture. So it has been suggested that they were in fact carved in the reign of James IV's son, and were 'ante-dated' by the latter as an act of piety to his father. Such a gesture would so clash with custom that it does not seem possible, and the Renaissance corbels must instead, in my view, indicate the advanced architectural taste within the reach of the Scottish king.

The Great Hall (**25**), measuring about 29 by 12.5m (95 by 40ft), is in other respects, too, an outward-looking building, as has been pointed out by Richard Fawcett. It had large rectangular windows on its long sides to north and south, divided by one mullion and one or two transoms. The form of the windows suggests an influence from France, where such windows are as much part of the architecture of the early Renaissance as they had been in the later Middle Ages. By contrast, the open hammerbeam roof of the Hall looks like a Scottish translation of an English idea. Hammerbeam roofs, more sophisticated than the Edinburgh Castle example, had been constructed for English kings – Richard II at Westminster, Edward IV at Eltham – and it is

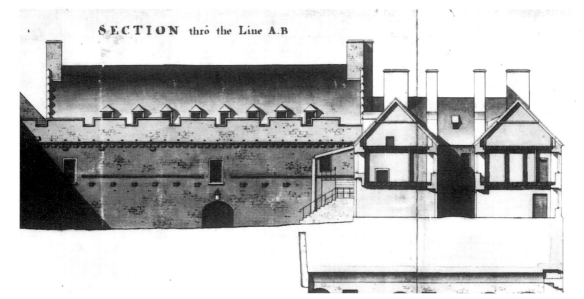

SECTION thro' the Line A.B

25 *The elevation of the Great Hall towards the principal courtyard as it appears in an accurate military survey of 1754. By this date it had been used as a barracks for a century, and there may have been earlier modifications. Nevertheless, apart from the segmental-arched entrance and the row of dormers behind the parapet, the exterior seems to be unaltered since the Hall was completed in the first years of the sixteenth century.*

apposite that this Scottish paraphrase welcomed an English princess to share the country's throne. The type of roof was still in high fashion in England, for the most sumptuous example was to be made at Hampton Court for James IV's brother-in-law when he became Henry VIII.

The Castle now stood at the summit of a many-faceted pre-eminence, above all other places in the realm; fortress, palace, arsenal, treasury, repository of the national archives, the residence of several officers of state including the Treasurer, and state prison. As state prison, it had provided a classic escape story in 1479, when James III's brother, Alexander, Duke of Albany, had been confined there on a charge of treason. Albany killed his guards and lowered himself down the face of the Rock by a rope fastened to his window. His companion slipped and injured

himself, but Albany resolutely carried him to Leith.

The Castle continued on this high plateau of prestige through the sixteenth century and into the next. Already in James IV's time, however, there were clear signs of fundamental change in its active functions. There is no evidence that Parliament ever sat in the new Great Hall in James's lifetime or later, for while the location of Parliament fixed itself more and more in Edinburgh, it met now in the Tolbooth or Town House. And the improvement of the Palace in the Castle may well have been for reasons of prestige rather than anticipated usefulness. It very soon began to decline in favour of the much more attractive Holyrood Abbey, with its new and reconstructed rooms of James IV.

In the Castle the most striking survivals from the reign of James IV are not only buildings but also Crown Jewels. In the early 1490s the Pope sent the King of Scots a Sceptre (26) and a golden rose as presents. It has been generally assumed that Alexander VI (Rodrigo Borgia) made the gift, but it has recently been suggested that it might possibly have come from Alexander's predecessor, Innocent VIII. The sides of the slender silver-gilt rod are engraved with thistles and fleurs-de-lis, grotesque masks, cups and foliage, and its head is completed by a globe of polished rock crystal and a pearl. The Sceptre is a masterwork of Renaissance craftsmanship, although its elegant simplicity was rather compromised by ornament added in the next reign. Equally outstanding as an Italian work of art is the Sword, also a Papal gift to James IV, presented by Julius II in 1507 (27). Its blade carries etchings of St Peter and St Paul, and the name 'Julius II'. All the etchings are infilled with

gold, and the finely worked pommel is of silver gilt. A scabbard and a sword belt were part of the gift and have also survived. The arms of Pope Julius (28) are enamelled on a plate attached to the scabbard, which is of wood covered with crimson silk velvet. The belt is of woven lace with a silver-gilt buckle. Apart from their adventures in the seventeenth century, these precious possessions have always been safeguarded in the Castle since they arrived in Scotland, at first as part of the Treasury which may have been located in the vaults below David's Tower, and today in the 'Crown Room', specially built in 1615.

Eventually the chief beneficiary of the slow process of change in the balance of the Castle's functions was to be the arsenal. It took over the old Great Hall (which has been envisaged on the summit of the Rock) as the Workhouse, and a

26 *In the foreground the Sceptre, sent to James IV as a gift by Pope Alexander VI (or just possibly by Alexander's predecessor Innocent VIII) lengthened and remodelled with figures of the Virgin and Child, St James and St Andrew at the order of James V; with it in this photograph are the other elements of the Regalia of Scotland, the Crown and the Sword.*

foundry was built in 1511, perhaps against the west rampart near the old Hall. The largest bronze guns could now be cast there. Robert Borthwick, James IV's Master Gunner, was also the master 'melter' or founder, casting ordnance bearing the legend *Machina sum Scoto Borthvik fabricata Roberto* ('I am an engine made by the Scot Robert Borthwick'). The contents of the arsenal were soon to be put to use. The political fruits of James IV's English match had promised a happy ending to more than two hundred years of conflict. Peace, however, did not long survive the succession of James's brother-in-law to the English throne as Henry VIII. The two self-willed monarchs clashed, and in the autumn of 1513 James IV's magnificent train of artillery (leaving behind the now old-fashioned Mons Meg) was hauled down the winding road from the Gunhouse for the campaign that ended at Flodden.

The Thistle and the Fleur-de-lis

After Flodden (1513), their king, with much of his army, dead on the battlefield, the Scots looked to France for support. They proposed the formal renewal of the Franco-Scottish alliance and invited John Stewart, Duke of Albany (resident in France and with all of his interests there, but close in succession to the Scottish throne) to come to Scotland as Governor on behalf of the infant James V. The resolution of most leading Scots to fight back against misfortune was stiffened by Henry VIII's action in claiming the right to be Protector of Scotland. In February 1514 Robert Borthwick, continuing in office as Master Gunner, was arranging with Albany's representative, le Sieur de la Bastie, to garrison and arm Edinburgh Castle. Both men planned new outworks to be made before the place on the Castle Hill, though we do not know how far this scheme of fortification proceeded. Albany arrived in Scotland in 1515. Dunbar Castle had been chosen as his principal base, and it received a French garrison with a powerful armament of French guns, while Edinburgh

27 *The sword sent to James IV as a present by Pope Julius II in 1507 and secured in the treasury of Edinburgh Castle. The Sword of State is still part of the Regalia of Scotland.*

continued as the chief Scottish arsenal and strongpoint.

Two years later James V was brought to the safety of the 'windy and right unpleasant castle and rock of Edinburgh', taken away on the suspicion that a child with an infectious disease had been in the place, then brought back to spend some time there with his tutor Gavin Dunbar, later the Archbishop of Glasgow. The climatic discomforts of the Castle as a residence are as much a refrain throughout its history as is its security.

The Castle did not figure largely in national affairs during James's minority, but his first act on assuming direct rule in 1528 was to take artillery from it for the siege of Tantallon, held

28 *Pope Julius II (Giuliano della Rovere); the portrait by Raphael.*

against him by his stepfather Archibald Douglas Earl of Angus, and this marks the beginning of his intense personal interest in the Castle's arsenal. Throughout his reign the gun foundry there continued in use under Robert Borthwick and his successors, the Frenchmen Peris and David Rowan. It cast guns of all sizes from cannon downward, though the only survivor from the period is a small 'falcon' (**29**) of 50mm (2in) bore with James V's arms and cipher (preserved in the Art Gallery and Museum of Glasgow). The old Hall, now the Workhouse, had machinery for boring out guns, and in 1539–40 St Mary's Church was converted into the Munition House. Two intermediate floors were inserted and the doors and windows were altered, with one or two of the doors large enough to bring the artillery train into the ground floor.

These changes were making parts of the Castle more like an industrial site than a place for gracious royal living, and James V's ambitious programme of palace building – at Holyrood, Falkland, Linlithgow and Stirling Castle – was not reflected at Edinburgh Castle's Palace. The latter was now receding further into the background as far as regular royal use was concerned, eclipsed as a residence convenient to

29 *A small piece of artillery called a falcon made for James V, and now in the Glasgow Art Gallery and Museum. It is the only survivor of large numbers of guns of all sizes made during James's reign. It may have been stored in the Castle arsenal, and perhaps was cast in the foundry there (the mounting is of much later date).*

IACOBVS · 5 · DEI GRATIA
REX ✝ SCOTORVM

M R

30 *James V (1513–42) and Mary of Guise.*

the capital by the newly transformed Holyrood, which was more to the advanced taste of both James and his French queen, Mary of Guise (**30**) than the 'right unpleasant' old stronghold. The only non-military work certainly known to have been built by James in the Castle was a new Register House, in 1540–2, on a site between his father's Great Hall and extended Palace. At about this time a new place of worship seems to have been built replacing St Margaret's Chapel, but the origins of this structure, altered several times and then demolished in the mid-nineteenth century, are vague in the extreme.

Turning to the Castle's contents, a good deal of royal interest was devoted to the regalia,

either already in or destined for the Scottish Treasury housed in the Castle. New ornaments were added in 1536 to the Sceptre presented to James's father, and it was lengthened. The Crown of Scotland was completely remade to take its existing form in 1540 by an Edinburgh goldsmith, John Mosman. Mosman himself supplied 23 stones for it; and stones and pearls from the old Crown enlarged its rich ornamentation (**colour plate 9**).

The Crown of Scotland survives as it was then made. Its lower part is a gold band, with 22 large cut and polished stones alternating with pearls. Above the band are settings of smaller stones from the old Crown, ten fleurs-de-lis and ten crosses fleury, the latter set with pearls. The four gold arches of the crown, ornamented with gold and red enamel oak leaves, bear a gold celestial globe enamelled in blue and sprinkled with gold stars. On top of the globe is a gold and black enamel cross, with pearls attached to its sides and a rectangular amethyst set in its centre. A bonnet for the Crown, of velvet and satin, was made in 1540 by Thomas Arthur – it is now shown with a modern crimson silk velvet bonnet trimmed with ermine (see **26**).

There now existed the complete regalia, the 'Honours of Scotland' that are still in the Castle today. The Honours were to be used for the coronations of James V's daughter Mary, of James VI, and the Scottish coronations of Charles I and Charles II. Much more frequently these symbols of royal authority were prominent in the ceremonies associated with the Scottish Parliament. Thus the Crown, Sword and Sceptre were taken from the Castle and borne by noblemen before the King for the opening of his Parliament in December 1540.

There is no evidence for new fortifications during James's personal reign, or of repair to, for example, provisional works that may have been thrown up on the Castle Hill immediately after Flodden. The Castle Hill, however, emerges with a grim prominence for its use as a place of public execution. In 1538 a nobleman was beheaded here and a few days later the sister of the Earl of Angus was burnt, on charges of high treason. The approach to the Castle was to become best known for the burning of witches, and those convicted of 'unnatural crimes'.

James died in December 1542 with the news of the sorry defeat of Solway Moss and was succeeded by his six-day-old daughter Mary, and James Hamilton, Earl of Arran became Regent. Henry VIII opened negotiations with Arran for a treaty stipulating the future marriage of the baby Queen of Scots and Henry's infant son Edward, Prince of Wales. After dragging on for some time the negotiations broke down, the Franco-Scottish alliance was revived and the piqued Henry launched an attack under the Earl of Hertford in May 1544. Parts of the town of Edinburgh, and parts also of Holyrood Abbey, were burnt. Hertford approached the Castle but

– perhaps because he lacked an adequate train of artillery – he did not seriously attempt to capture it. The Scots were alarmed about the security of the place; we do not know what may have been done in the years just after Flodden, but it is most likely that no important defences had been built since the 1380s. Substantial works were begun on new fortifications in July 1544. The work went on (and its objectives seem to have become more ambitious) against a background of inter-mittent war, which although it did not reach Edinburgh again was nevertheless sufficiently threatening. Henry VIII's death in 1547 did not relieve the pressure. Hertford in his new style of Duke of Somerset, Lord Protector of England for Edward VI, invaded in September 1547, defeat-ing the Scots at Pinkie and building strongpoints in East Lothian and Berwickshire with the apparent intention of keeping an occupying force in south-east Scotland until an Anglo-Scottish royal marriage was assured. Somerset's plans were upset by a French expeditionary force which landed at Leith in June 1548 and laid siege to the strongest of the new English forts at Haddington, while the whole purpose of Somer-set's invasion evaporated with Scottish agree-ment that Mary Queen of Scots should marry the Dauphin of France, and Mary's voyage to France in July.

Peace was made with England in 1550. By that time the works at Edinburgh Castle begun in 1544 may have been completed, though some of them were not paid for until 1552. To the east there was now a new and massive rampart, loopholed for the heaviest artillery extending from David's Tower to the Constable's Tower. The line of this rampart is preserved today in the Forewall Battery. Above it was an upper level of gun positions between the Munition House and

31 *Henri II of France (1547–59), the father-in-law of Mary Queen of Scots. He sent an engineer to Scotland to improve the defences of Edinburgh Castle.*

St Margaret's Chapel. Below it was an angular work pushed forward on to the Castle Hill, designed by an Italian engineer – probably Migliorino Ubaldini, just sent to Scotland by Henri II of France, the host and prospective father-in-law of the Queen of Scots (**31**). The Spur, as it was later called, attempted to apply some of the principles of the 'new fortification' (originating in Italy, and only now introduced to Britain) to an awkward site. There may in addition have been other new defences around the perimeter, giving the Castle more capability for defence by and against artillery, even though it was unsuited to the symmetrical plans based on the angle bastion that had been pioneered in Italy. The Spur was reckoned effective enough to be rebuilt after it was destroyed in the siege of 1573, and an altered version of its northern flank defence still exists today (with the march of time, its interior is now part of the Castle gift shop).

The continuing French interest in Scotland was reinforced when Mary of Guise, the widowed queen of James V, became Regent in succession to Arran (by then created Duke of Châtelhérault in France), and even more in 1558 when Mary Queen of Scots (**32**) married the Dauphin who succeeded to the French throne as François II on 10 July 1559. But François died only seventeen months later, and during this time the French position of strength in Scotland disintegrated. The revolutionary reform of the Scottish church had already begun, and in October 1559 the Protestant leaders, the Lords of the Congregation, announced the deposition of the Regent and asked Elizabeth of England for help. An English fleet was followed in March 1560 by an English army. Suffering from a fatal illness, Mary of Guise left Holyrood on 1 April and was received by the Keeper, Lord Erskine, into Edinburgh Castle where she died. Her lead coffin lay in the Castle under a pall with a cross of white taffeta until September, when permission was at last granted by the Lords of the Congregation to carry it to France to be buried in the Abbey of St Pierre at Reims. Meanwhile, with no one to represent the Crown, a Scottish Parlia-

32 Bust of Mary Queen of Scots by Ponce Jacquio, wearing the closed French crown as Queen of France, 1559–60.

ment had taken it upon itself to abolish Roman Catholicism, and an Anglo-French treaty provided for the withdrawal of the foreign armies.

Queen Mary's fortress

The ships bringing Mary Stuart and her little train back to Scotland came to harbour at Leith on 19 August 1561 after a misty voyage from Calais. The 18-year-old Queen of Scots, widow of François II of France, was conducted to the Abbey of Holyrood, which was to be her chief residence, about half a mile outside the town gates of Edinburgh. The Palace there was not as spacious as those she had left in her late husband's kingdom but, as rebuilt by her father James V, it was far from uncomfortable or old-fashioned, and it had attractive surroundings of ornamental gardens and a mountainous hunting-park. A ceremonial Royal Visit to the Scottish capital was planned for a fortnight later.

33 This reconstruction sketch shows the Castle as it might have appeared at the time of Mary Queen of Scots' first visit in 1561 after her return from France. The Spur is in the left foreground. (Drawing by Dave Pollock.)

It was to be staged for maximum effect with Mary emerging from her principal strength, the Castle, and descending the Castle Hill to enter Edinburgh, rather having the procession climbing the long slope through the Canongate from Holyrood (33).

So it was arranged that she was first to dine at the Castle, and early in the morning of 2 September the Queen rode out of Holyrood accompanied by virtually all of the nobility of Scotland. The cavalcade skirted the city by a country road round the Nor' Loch (more or less the line today occupied by Princes Street), turned near St Cuthbert's Church and ascended the steep path to the west postern. There is enough evidence to attempt some reconstruction of what might be seen on the way to the Castle's Palace above the south-eastern precipices of the Rock. Just inside the postern, by the archery butts, were emplaced some of the guns of the powerful armament of the place: an extra large cannon of 205mm (8in) bore, a long-range *culverin*, next in

size below a cannon, and two other pieces. Approaching the summit there was the gun foundry built for Mary's grandfather, once capable of casting the heaviest artillery, but shut down since the 1550s, and on the right there was visible the back of the Gunhouse, another arsenal building of James IV. Entering the summit citadel, there was on the left the old Great Hall which may have dated back to before the Wars of Independence, now the Workhouse for the arsenal. Beyond it stood a recently-built chapel which would now have been adapted for the use of the Protestant Kirk; this structure continued in use well into the nineteenth century as the garrison chapel. With the construction of this building, David I's St Margaret's Chapel had gone out of ecclesiastical use and it may already have been turned into a magazine either for gunpowder or for arsenal stores. Finally the inner court, Palace Yard, had a continuing emphasis on the sinews of war. To the west was the Gunhouse which the party had already seen from below, while to the north the medieval St Mary's Church was now the Munition House.

At all times Palace Yard was to some extent insulated from the noisy, smoky and dirty activities of the arsenal, for the working entrances to the Gunhouse and the Munition House did not lead from the Yard itself. These activities would no doubt be respectfully stilled on the occasion of the Royal Visit, for which the Palace and the Great Hall would have been made ready. Except for special events the interior of the Palace would be almost unfurnished. Now tapestries would be hung on the walls and woven matting laid on the floors; there would be benches for the guests, a sideboard-buffet for silver plates and cups, trestles and boards to form the tables, with damask tablecloths to cover them. A special table (not just a board on trestles) would be provided for the Queen, who would have the only chair in the room under a Canopy of State and with a Cloth of State hung behind it.

So at 12 noon Mary dined with her aristocracy, together with John Erskine, Keeper of the Castle since the mid-1550s and very soon to be created Earl of Mar. After the dinner the party left Palace Yard and descended from the summit by the winding roadway engineered to move the artillery train in and out of the Castle, passing by the Constable's Tower and beneath the shadows of the Forewall and David's Tower to enter the Spur, the modern Italian-designed fortification still not quite finished. The guns fired a salute as the Queen of Scots left her fortress, to be met on the Castle Hill by a party of fifty young men gaudily dressed up as Moors, decked with costume jewellery, their faces, arms and legs blackened, introducing the lavish welcome contrived by the burgh.

During the six years of Mary's personal reign the buildings and fortifications of the Castle remained much as they had been during the Regency. The Spur may never have been completed with a massive parapet as intended, though the emplaced armament was further strengthened. In 1562 a 75mm (3in) piece was hoisted to the top of David's Tower, and in 1565 four 165mm ($6\frac{1}{2}$in) cannon brought from France were mounted on the Forewall of the east front. By 1566 the ramparts of the perimeter bristled with at least 25 cast-bronze guns. Besides the new French cannon the Forewall had two *great culverins*, and above and behind the Forewall, between the Munition House and the building that had been St Margaret's Chapel, was a second tier of eastward facing emplacements with two *bastard culverins* and two more cannon. On the north front were two cannon and two 75mm (3in) guns; four pieces as we have noticed at and near the west postern; four more guns along the south front along with a great culverin and a 75mm (3in) gun next to the Great Hall beside the Gunhouse gable. Two of the culverins had been captured from England, but a number of the other guns had probably been manufactured in the Castle while the foundry was working.

Besides the artillery of position, the Castle held a great variety of munitions of war, some of it stored rather haphazardly. Most was kept in

34 *These stone panels showing artillery, including Mons Meg, and other munitions of war were carved in the 1600s and were originally placed on one of the buildings of the arsenal in the castle. They are now set in the passage of the Victorian Entrance Gateway.*

the three storeys of the Munition House, with more in the Gunhouse, the Workhouse, a small store above the forge and in the Powder Vault (possibly, as noted, St Margaret's Chapel). There was only a limited number of the bigger guns in store, for all the large cast bronze muzzle-loaders of modern design were emplaced in the open. The ancient Mons Meg was elsewhere, perhaps at Holyrood – the abbey-palace was not entirely devoted to peaceful pursuits for it sometimes accommodated a small artillery park. There were only eight forged iron pieces kept under cover in the Castle, long *serpentines* and lighter *cut-throats*, and along with these there were 136 handguns.

For the artillery, there were carriages and parts of carriages to mount various sizes of gun, wooden trestles for mounting handguns, mops for sponging them out, brass chargers for loading them with powder and handspikes to elevate and depress them; 200 yokes for the oxen that pulled the train on campaign, heavy ropes and cables, two of the special guncarts with shields for use on the battlefield, 23 enclosed carts to transport powder and shot; bullet moulds, lead chain shot and other shot, some of it kept in barrels. The Powder Vault held 66 barrels of gunpowder, with 17 more barrels in the Munition House. There were 700 pikes, six crossbows, old breastplates and backplates, with more modern armour in the French fashion and horse armour; and picks and shovels for the pioneers.

While, as already noted, the fortress-arsenal was not the most gracious, comfortable or even salubrious of royal residences, it did offer security along with prestige in abundance, and so the Privy Council chóse the Castle as the location where the heir to the throne was to be born 'if it may stand with the Queen's Majesty's pleasure and the health of her body'. Mary had married her cousin Henry Stewart, Lord Darnley, eldest son of the Earl of Lennox, in July 1565 and was expecting King Henry's child – he was given the royal style after the marriage – in June 1566. The love-match had led to a most unhappy marriage, and the courts of Europe had been shocked by the conspiracy to murder David Rizzio set up by King Henry, when Mary herself had been threatened by a pistol held by one of the conspirators, Andrew Ker of Fawdonside.

Mary took up residence in the Palace of the Castle in April in the great suite that had been fashioned by her grandfather, James IV. There she had the century-old Great Chamber, presumably where she had dined just after her return to Scotland as described above; a large Inner Chamber which was, following contemporary etiquette, both reception room and bedroom; and an innermost small private room called the Cabinet, occupying a similar place in the room sequence to the Holyrood Cabinet where her fateful supper-party with a small company including her secretary David Rizzio had been held. It is interesting to note that, while the private Lodgings in David's Tower presumably still existed, Mary did not use the Queen's Lodging there, but for the great occasion of the birth of an heir to the throne resided in this more ample suite. Other accommodation might be vacated to provide some lodging for the Queen's retinue, but there was not sufficient space for the whole Court, as there was at Holyrood.

The Inner Chamber was richly furnished with a bed hung with blue velvet and blue taffeta, though the birth took place in the cramped seclusion of the Cabinet. Between 10 and 11 in the morning of Wednesday 19 June, 1566 a baby prince was born to the Queen of Scots. The powerful armament fired a salute, and five hundred bonfires were lit in the town. The birth had been difficult, and it was rumoured that the Countess of Atholl had used witchcraft to transfer the pains of labour to a complaisant lady-in-waiting. But not too long afterwards Mary was able to receive, with the infant taken from his cradle, wrapped in ten ells of Holland cloth and displayed as a healthy child. She was being visited by King Henry and others when an uncomfortable and disquieting conversation was alleged to have taken place:

'My Lord, God has given you and me a son, begotten by none but you!' At which words the King blushed, and kissed the child. Then she took the child in her arms, and said:
'My Lord, here I protest to God, and as I shall answer to Him at the great day of judgement, this is your son, and no other man's son.'

Mary went on from her child's legitimacy to the night of Rizzio's murder and the estrangement between the royal couple that followed, voicing her suspicion that if Andrew Ker had fired and killed her and her unborn child – which she darkly implied might have been an intended part of the plot – Henry would have seized the opportunity to assume the rank and title of King of Scots in his own right.

'Madam,' answered the King, 'these things are past.'
'Then,' said the Queen, 'let them go!'

Many people felt that Mary could not let these ugly things of the past go, and when King Henry was murdered in the following year, it was rumoured that she had encouraged the conspiracy. The rumour hardened to firm belief when it became clear that she was going to marry Henry's reputed killer, James Hepburn, Earl of Bothwell. When the Queen next entered the Castle, on 6 May 1567, Bothwell – newly created Duke of Orkney – led her horse by the bridle up to the Castlehill. Mary stayed in the Castle until the marriage was celebrated at Holyrood on 11 May. The catastrophe soon followed: surrender at Carberry Hill, abdication, escape from Lochleven, the battle at Langside and flight to England.

On Mary's abdication, James Balfour of

Pittendreich as Keeper had allowed the Honours of Scotland to be taken from the Castle to Stirling for the coronation of her son as James VI of Scotland on 29 July 1567. Balfour, however, was soon replaced by the Regent, Mary's illegitimate half-brother, the Earl of Moray. Moray appointed Sir William Kirkcaldy of Grange as Keeper to maintain the interest of the king's party in the chief fortress of the country. The Regent Moray was assassinated in January 1570, but even before that Kirkcaldy had shown some leanings towards the party of the exiled queen, who still retained the support of a formidable opposition. The hindsight of history gives a finality to Mary's forced abdication in 1567 which it did not have to contemporaries, and the Castle became a constant and worrying reminder to the ruling group that its power

might be subverted. By the middle of 1571 Kirkcaldy was openly supporting Mary's cause, sending the Honours of Scotland to her party on the occasion of its rival Parliament in Edinburgh (while the Parliament convened in Stirling by the king's party had to make do with an imitation set of regalia), and receiving money and war material from Mary's brother-in-law from her first marriage, Charles IX of France.

35 *A contemporary impression of the siege of Edinburgh Castle in 1573, from Raphael Holinshed's* Chronicles. *The Anglo-Scottish batteries ringing the stronghold are clearly shown, including that on the Castle Hill directing its fire on the Spur and David's Tower and the upper defences to the north of David's Tower.*

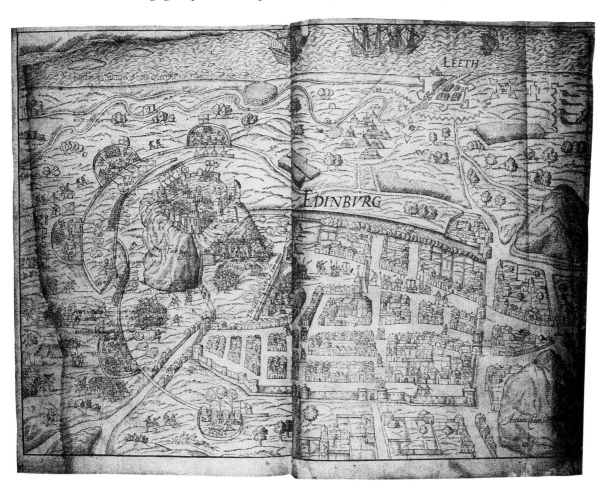

After Moray's death the Regency was held in rapid succession by the Earl of Lennox who was killed in a skirmish, the Earl of Mar who died naturally, and then by the capable and ruthless James Douglas, Earl of Morton. He opened a siege of the Castle, but since the best Scottish artillery was inside the fortress, the investment went on inconclusively until help from Queen Elizabeth of England was sought in 1573. In January of that year an English reconnaissance party surveyed the Castle, giving a detailed account of its formidable defences and weaponry, which seems to have been unchanged

36 *The east elevation of the Palace today shows the corbels and bases of James IV's magnificent oriel windows destroyed in the siege.*

37 *James VI at about six years old, by Arnold van Brounckhurst. The portrait was painted about a year before the devastating siege of Edinburgh Castle in 1573, when the stronghold was captured from the supporters of James's exiled mother Mary Stuart.*

since the state of its deployment in 1566 already described, and adding:

> ... We find that there is no mining that can prevail in this rock but only battery with ordnance to beat down the walls and so to make the climb ...

In April ships arrived at Leith with an English force and a sufficient siege train, commanded by Sir William Drury, Governor of Berwick upon Tweed. The Anglo-Scottish besiegers set up six batteries. One was at the head of the built-up

area of the Castlehill confronting the eastern defences, two towards the south, the fourth on the high ground near St Cuthbert's Church, the fifth and sixth on the north side using the ridge now followed by Princes Street. A devastating fire was opened on 16 May. Kirkcaldy seems to have had adequate provisions, though the water supply was less than plentiful and was critically reduced when the principal well was choked by the partial collapse of David's Tower, which had begun to disintegrate two days before. The whole front from David's Tower to the Constable's Tower, and the Spur advanced from the front, were systematically shot to pieces, and a successful assault was made on the Spur. On 29 May the Castle was surrendered. Some of the principal members of the garrison, including Kirkcaldy and his brother, were hanged. William Maitland of Lethington, once Queen Mary's secretary, died in prison in Leith, perhaps by suicide. The fall of the Castle did not extinguish support for the exiled queen, but it marked a turning-point in the firm establishment of the new regime in power.

CHAPTER FOUR

Double Crowns

King James's peace

The reconstruction of the Castle after the siege of 1573 seems to have been largely carried out in the remaining part of the Earl of Morton's first term of office as Regent, from 1572 to 1578 (**38**). On the principal east front, the shattered Spur with its flank defences was restored, apparently to much the same plan as before, while the overall concept of the works behind the Spur was substantially revised. A great rounded defence, the Half-Moon (**39**), was wrapped around the lower storeys of the ruins of David's Tower, and the latter disappeared from view inside and under the new masonry (**40**). The Forewall was reconstructed northward from the Half-Moon to a new gate-tower – replacing the Constable's Tower – with a portcullis (it was later given the name Portcullis Gate (see **41**), and that name will be used here from now on). Although the parapets of the Half-Moon and the Forewall took their present shape at the end of the seventeenth century, and an entirely new tower-like structure was put on top of the Porcullis Gate in the 1880s, the fortifications behind the Spur retain today the forms that they were given during Morton's Regency, and have a significant place in the general history of fortification in Scotland, as well as in the story of Edinburgh Castle, whose visual impact they transformed.

As already noted, attempts had been made to adapt the east front of the Castle to the demands of the age of artillery in the construction of the

38 *James Douglas, fourth Earl of Morton (d. 1581), Regent of Scotland from 1572 to 1578. He reduced Edinburgh Castle with English help in 1573 and initiated major repairs to the siege damage.*

Spur together with the emplacement of guns at a higher level, on top of David's Tower and north of it. The operations of the 1570s took the process to a comprehensive conclusion. The rounded form of the Half-Moon descends from a long line of thinking on artillery fortification (the best-known name associated with rounded strongpoints is that of Albrecht Dürer, who wrote an important, pioneering book on fortification in 1527); the form was obsolescent by the late sixteenth century save for difficult sites such as Edinburgh. There, it allowed for a battery of numerous guns giving a wide horizontal sweep of fire in this narrow rock-girt location where the mainstream ideas of contemporary military engineering based on the angle bastion could not be applied. The Half-Moon's firepower was augmented by that of the guns of the Forewall at the same level – a uniform level for the main fighting platform of a front is one of the features that distinguishes artillery fortifications from the high towers and much lower curtains of medieval defences. The new works retained the single embrasure at a lower level for a heavy gun to fire on fixed lines down the Castle Hill. The opening was blocked in 1695, during the repairs after the siege six years earlier, when the parapets above were redesigned as they now appear.

Apart from string-courses that break and progressively reduce the diameter of the great mass of its battered (sloping) walls, the rubble masonry of the Half-Moon is quite plain. In this it contrasts with the ornamental detail of the Portcullis Gate. Such a contrast between main gates and the defensive elements of the perimeter may be seen throughout the development of artillery fortification until well into the nineteenth century. William McDowell, Master of Work, was paid for the building of the gate in

40 *The Half-Moon Battery. In spite of damage inflicted after it was built in the course of three sieges, the only significant alteration from the first design is the parapet (of the 1690s).*

39 *The Half-Moon Battery during the course of its building after the 1573 siege, wrapped around (and so concealing) the ruins of David's Tower. Left, the damaged Palace; behind David's Tower, the Munition House; right, the new Portcullis Gate; foreground, the devastated Spur. (Drawing by David Simon.)*

December 1577. As far as its provisions for security were concerned, it had two outer doors and an inner door as well as the portcullis. The latter did not have any protection in the low gate structure where upper works were not at first provided. The ornamental part of the Gate uses Renaissance detail with flair, enhanced perhaps by a lack of full scholarly understanding. The segmental arch is flanked by slim pilasters above which lions crouch gazing at an aedicule – a little blind opening with a pediment and Ionic order – which presumably always contained a shield with the royal arms, though the present one dates only from 1887 (41).

Since the abdication of his mother in 1567, the young King James VI had spent most of his life at Stirling, where the castle offered reasonable

security from intrusion by the enemies of the party that guarded him. In the summer and autumn of 1579, at the age of thirteen, James made a tour of the east of Scotland and on 17 October made a ceremonial entry into Edinburgh on the occasion of his first formal visit to the city. Works at the Castle were still in part incomplete, and indeed five years later the King, 'understanding how his Castle of Edinburgh, where his principal jewels, movables, munitions and registers are kept, since the last storming thereof is destitute of sundry necessary fortifications ... to the great danger of the same Castle' instructed Chancellor Arran, who was also Captain of the Castle and had a lodging there, to inspect the place and repair it. The Portcullis Gate was now, in 1584, at last completed under the direction of William Schaw. Two storeys were added, giving much-needed protection to the portcullis which in the short space of time since its erection had rusted badly in the open, and also creating new accommodation for Arran as Captain. Parts of the defences and some internal buildings, however, were still in disrepair in 1588. Even in recent times the works organization has never been able completely to keep pace with deterioration through the wide area over which the stronghold extends.

James's concern with the Castle was as his 'first and principal strength of the realm' rather than as a palace, for his Edinburgh residence was Holyrood. The remodelled defences of his principal strength were not, however, to be put to the test in his long reign. After the turmoil of the last phase of Mary's reign and through the regencies, the country gradually became more stable and

42 *James VI of Scotland and I of England, by Paul van Somer. Painted in England, and showing the King holding the badge of the Garter in his right hand, and resting his left on a table with the English Crown Jewels. The date of the portrait is either 1615, when preparations had begun for James's 'Homecoming' to Scotland, or 1618, soon after his return to the south.*

41 *The Portcullis Gate which replaced the fourteenth-century Constable's Tower ruined in the 1573 siege, and which may just possibly incorporate some of the masonry of the latter. The lower part of the gate was finished by 1577; like the Half-Moon it was built during the regency of the Earl of Morton and has sometimes been called Morton's Gate. The upper part is an addition of the 1880s.*

settled, and from the 1590s dates the period that has been called 'King James's Peace'. The comparative tranquillity was not only internal, for relations with England improved under a ruler who had an intuitive understanding of politics. There were of course tensions and stresses between the two countries and no observer would confidently have dismissed the idea of conflict. With time, however, it was clear that Elizabeth of England would not have children and that James VI of Scotland – descended from Elizabeth's grandfather through the 1503 Anglo-Scottish Royal marriage – would on her death peacefully succeed to the throne of the 'Auld Enemy'. So in 1603 James set out for London to become also James I of England.

The Crowns were united, and James optimistically called his realms 'Great Britain'; but Scotland was as before an entirely separate state from her southern neighbour. She was governed by the Chancellor and Privy Council for the absent king, who appointed Commissioners to hold Scottish Parliaments on his behalf. Many of these activities of government were centred on Holyrood and the Tolbooth where Parliament met, though some official business might be carried on at the Castle. Yet the outstanding role of the latter as the national stronghold and arsenal, the location of the Treasury and the Scottish records, remained unchanged – the Honours of Scotland being taken from the Treasury to precede the Commissioner, representing the monarch, for Parliamentary ceremony, a ritual that only came to an end in 1707 with the Treaty of Union.

When he left Scotland, James had promised to return soon and often, but in the event the royal 'Homecoming' did not take place until 1617 and the visit was not repeated. Well in advance, programmes of work were begun at the Castle, at Holyrood and elsewhere. The Abbey, as it was still called, was intended to be, as before, the principal royal residence, but the Castle was to play a significant supporting role. Stone quarried at Inverleith, lime from Kirkliston and sand were carted up the Castle Hill and the 'founding drink' was handed out to the masons on 14 March 1615. Work was carried out on the walls, which were repaired and harled (a particular kind of roughcast finish). This was done standing on ladders or hung in a cradle: above the crags it could be a perilous task for which the masons were paid danger money. Inside the Castle, the forge and the Munition House were repaired, and the sixteenth-century Chapel

(beside St Margaret's Chapel now part of the arsenal) was re-roofed.

The most important building operation, however, was the refurbishment and part-reconstruction of the Palace, carried out between 1615 and 1616. The King's master mason William Wallace was in charge of the operation, though it has been suggested that the Master of Works, James Murray, may have been responsible for the design. The most conspicuous change was the contriving of a tower-like superstructure on the rectangular block that had its origins as the fifteenth-century Great Chamber. The importance of this 'tower' was heavily underlined. It had a battlemented parapet with prominent cannon waterspouts, at the east corners towards the town there were corbelled-out square turrets with ogee leaded roofs, and on its east and north sides there were panels and pediments carved with royal emblems, including the Honours of Scotland. The entrance to its two upper storeys, one of which was entirely new and the other remodelled, was by a new round-arched door with emphatic rusticated quoins in an advanced architectural idiom. Above the door is a cartouche with the monogram MAH and the date 1566, representing the initials of James VI's parents, Mary and Henry, and the year of the king's birth (**43**).

While the documentary evidence relating to the renovated Palace is not at first sight at all clear on the functions of the rooms in this 'tower', a closer analysis establishes that the suites on its east side (the side given such emphasis by conspicuous ornament) were designed as a personal Royal Lodging for James VI with, above it, an identical Lodging for the queen (though in the event Anne of Denmark was not to accompany her husband in 1617). The entry to the suites from the courtyard is given parallel emphasis by its striking new door and the MAH inscription.

The newly-built Royal Lodgings have close similarities in their arrangement and sequence of rooms to those that had existed at Holyrood from the late 1520s and with which James VI was

43 *The entry to the new Royal Lodgings built in 1615–16 has above it the cipher 'MAH' for Mary and Henry, the parents of James VI, and '1566', the year when he was born.*

familiar from his residence there up to 1603. Each has an Antechamber – a room for living in, for dining and for less formal audience; a Bedchamber – not just for sleeping in, but an audience chamber as well; and as the most secluded and private place in the suite, a Closet or Cabinet, where the monarch might secretly discuss matters of state, and also enjoy himself with cronies without disturbance. (Edinburgh had one Cabinet, while Holyrood unusually had two – one of them very famous as the scene of the little supper party held by Mary Queen of Scots

from which David Rizzio was dragged away and murdered.) None of the three rooms in these personal royal suites at Edinburgh is large: the biggest are the Bedchambers, measuring around 6.6 by 7.6m (22 by 25ft). With the construction of this accommodation, the Castle again had the normal complement of separate private suites for the king and queen, which it had lost in 1573 when the Royal Lodgings in David's Tower were destroyed, along with the tower, in the siege.

Separate from the King's Lodging but adjoining it, a floor was added to the south which apparently provided a new suite seemingly comprising a Hall – another room for dining, in less private style, and also at this time a station of the ceremonial Palace Guard, hence its later name of the Guard Hall – and a Presence

44 *A detail of the birthplace of James VI.*

Chamber which, as its name implies, was primarily intended as a room of formal audience, though it too might also be used for dining. Such a pattern resembles that of the 1530s west range at Holyrood. From now on the old hall in the Palace is called the 'Laigh [lower] Hall' (it now has the recent name of the King's Dining Room), and in 1617, together with the rest of the old suite on the ground floor of the Palace, it seems to have been intended as a distinguished set of rooms which included the little Cabinet where James VI had been born.

The birthplace seems to have been regarded, and decorated, as a secular shrine for which it is not easy to think of parallels (**44–5**). While the ancient panelled timber ceiling does not seem to have been altered, the room was transformed by one John Anderson, who was paid the very large sum of one hundred pounds Scots in June 1617 for 'painting the room where His Majesty was

born and for furnishing gold colours and workmanship'. The painting, though restored, survives. On the ceiling there are thistles and the crowned ciphers IR and MR for *Iacobus Rex* and *Maria Regina*, the King and his mother. On the frieze is '19 Iunii', '1566', and the Royal Arms of Scotland with a little verse in old Scots that begins:

> Lord Jesu Chryst that Crounit was with thornse
> Preserve the Birth quhais Badgie heir is borne.

Exceptionally, the couplet is here quoted in its original spelling because otherwise it loses all of its Doric effectiveness.

As a further part of the preparations for the Homecoming, in May 1617 the neglected Mons Meg was raised out of the ground and prepared with the other ordnance for a welcoming salute.

45 *The little chamber where James VI was born on 19 June 1566, redecorated as a secular shrine for James's 'Homecoming' in 1617.*

Wooden figures of St George and the dragon were carved to be drawn in procession, and a pair of gloves made for St George. Blue ribbons were tied to the gates for the entry of the king. During almost all of his stay in Scotland from May until August 1617, however, James was elsewhere, particularly at Holyrood. The Palace in the Castle was pre-eminently a symbolic element in the pomp and circumstance of the visit, rather than a building to be used by the monarch. Most of the Court stayed in the Abbey, though the Earl of Buckingham, the King's favourite and also his Master of Horse, lodged in the Castle in the uppermost suite of Palace rooms there, which had apparently been provided for the Queen as has already been noted.

The reign of James VI saw a transformation in the visual impact of the Castle from the east

46 *The ornate plasterwork of the Castle's Palace as remodelled in 1615–16 has all been stripped out. This contemporary ceiling at Winton House in East Lothian is believed closely to resemble its style. (From Robert W. Billings,* Baronial and Ecclesiastical Antiquities of Scotland, *1845–52.)*

which endures to the present day: in his infancy with a major construction for war in the Half-Moon, and in his maturity with one for peace in the 'tower' of the Palace. The latter was rebuilt for a unique occasion, for James did not return to Scotland again.

> The world which late was golden with thy breath
> Is iron turned, and horrid, by thy death

lamented William Drummond of Hawthornden in 1625, using the conventionally high-flown language appropriate when writing about the decease of kings. It emerged, however, that Drummond's gloomy comment was exactly true.

Covenant and English conquest

Charles I, succeeding to the thrones of England and Scotland in 1625, did not travel north for his coronation as King of Scots until 1633 (**48**). Parliament was to meet during the visit, and the Town Council of Edinburgh was induced by the king to build a new Parliament House beside the old Tolbooth which had hitherto accommodated the assembly. Holyrood and the Castle were made ready for the occasion, although necessary repairs such as the new windows put into the Great Hall during May and June of 1633 left the outward appearance of the Castle as it

had been since the visit of Charles's father in 1617. While it is probable that the arrangement of rooms in the Castle's Palace was modified in a way better to reflect contemporary demands of etiquette for the coronation visit, the changes might have been made for Charles's last journey to Scotland in 1641.

Charles resided in Holyrood, but the Castle was to play a conspicuous part in the prologue to

47 The location of buildings constructed up to 1625 which survive above ground in a recognizable form, highlighted on a drawing of the twentieth-century castle: St Margaret's Chapel (1); the early part of the Portcullis Gate finished by 1577 (2); the Half-Moon begun and the Forewall reconstructed soon after 1573 (3) – their present parapets were formed in the 1690s; the Palace remodelled 1615–16 (4); the Great Hall completed in the early 1500s (5). The overall massing of the south-east front of the Castle has changed little since.

48 *Charles I at his coronation as King of Scotland, 1633.*

ecclesiastical grievances as the spearhead of political opposition. Charles neither negotiated nor prepared any effective countervailing force, and when civil war erupted in the following year the Covenanters' general, Alexander Leslie, was able to take Edinburgh Castle in March 1639 with little resistance from the unready garrison. At last Charles negotiated, and the Castle was restored to him by terms agreed at Berwick upon Tweed.

The Pacification of Berwick, as it became known, gave only a temporary respite. The Covenanters stayed under arms and war broke out again in 1640. Again Leslie invested the Castle, held – and better provided – by Lord Ettrick as Governor. Leslie placed his batteries much as Drury had done in 1573, again concentrating his fire against the critically important east front. Ettrick's powers of retaliation were

49 *The ampulla which held the consecrated oil used at the Scottish coronation of Charles I.*

the coronation. In England the monarch by custom spent the night before being crowned in his principal fortress, the Tower of London. Charles imported the idea to his northern realm, feasting in the Great Hall of the Castle and spending the night before the ceremony in the Palace there. The Honours were then carried in solemn procession to Holyrood, where the coronation took place (**49**).

The visit took place amid mounting discontent over constitutional, economic and church issues. Charles was not more obstinate than his father in trying to get his own way, but entirely lacked James VI's grasp of politics as the art of the possible. The powerful movement of dissent in Scotland gained cohesion with the signing of the Covenant in 1638, developing the issue of limited because of the damage his guns might do to the town, but he held out against bombardment until famine obliged him to surrender. Ettrick marched out with the honours of war on 15 September 1640 leaving the Castle, and particularly the Spur which had borne the brunt of Leslie's main batteries, badly damaged. The length of the 1640 siege contrasts with the thirteen days of investment in 1573, a difference that may be explained by several factors, though the stoutness of the defence was certainly no less in the earlier siege. The fortifications had been improved by the addition of more high-level ordnance on the platform of the Half-Moon Battery, perhaps giving as many as nine extra weapons; and it is likely that Leslie's siege train was less well-provided than Drury's. But certainly the fall of the place did not reflect adversely on the fortifications in an age when a very sophisticated military science of the attack and defence of places was developing.

The army of the Covenant moved to occupy the north of England, Charles softened his position and after long exchanges a treaty was concluded in June 1641. The King revisited Scotland in the autumn in an atmosphere very different from his coronation visit – though even then the clouds were beginning to form – and resided for most of his short stay in Holyrood. (The possibility has been noted that work may have been carried out to improve the intercommunication of rooms in the Palace in 1641, rather than in 1633.)

In August 1642 the outbreak of hostilities between the English Parliament and Charles threw Anglo-Scottish relations into confusion and further complicated the internal situation in Scotland. Until that time the Covenanters had been able to keep up a more or less united front, but the threat to 'their' king from English rebels reawakened traditional loyalties in many Scots who had opposed Charles on political and religious issues north of the Border. Civil war in Scotland reopened in 1644–5 with the Marquis of Montrose leading an army for Charles, and policy emerging from Scotland veered erratically

between support of the English Parliament and support of the King. The so-called Engagement with Charles took a Scottish army to England and to defeat by Oliver Cromwell at Preston in October 1648. Those leaders of the Covenanters who had opposed the Engagement then formed a new government, and met Cromwell as an ally in Edinburgh, perhaps in the Castle.

In the middle of this extreme crisis were produced the important drawings of Edinburgh, by James Gordon of Rothiemay, including a 'bird's-eye view' of the Castle (50). Most of the fortifications and buildings shown on the 1647 drawing are simple enough to identify: in particular, there is an invaluable record of the rebuilt Spur, and of the structures around the principal courtyard. In a most striking way, too, the drawing shows the lack of development on the Rock outside the area of the summit itself. In some respects the drawing is puzzling, for one might expect it to show St Margaret's Chapel beside the later chapel, but in fact only one building appears. On the Castle hill, below the Spur, the drawing shows a gallows, since this was still a place of execution in active use. From the beginning of the century most of the victims on the hill had been witches put to death by burning. The diarist John Nicol records that on 9 March 1659 'there were five women, witches, burnt on the Castle Hill for witchcraft, all of them confessing their covenanting with Satan, some of them renouncing their baptism, all of them often dancing with the Devil'.

The Anglo-Scottish accord collapsed when the English Parliament executed Charles I and established a republican Commonwealth in 1649. While the Scots had opposed Charles they certainly did not agree with this drastic outcome; still divided into armed factions, they proclaimed his son as Charles II. Cromwell (51) retaliated in 1650 with an invasion of Scotland, defeating the Scots at Dunbar and laying siege to the Castle. Cromwell's tactics resembled those used by Leslie, and again after a three months' investment the Castle surrendered on 24 December. The Regalia, the 'Honours of

Scotland', had been removed before the siege by the Marquis of Argyle and taken first to Perth, then to the Highlands, and so the ancient insignia could be used for the coronation of Charles II at Scone on New Year's Day 1651. The Honours were subsequently concealed from the invaders in a tale of adventure which took the precious objects to Dunnottar Castle on the wild coast of Kincardineshire and then, hidden in seaweed gathered by a servant girl, to the manse of the nearby church of Kinneff. In the manse,

the story alleges, they were temporarily kept at the bottom of the minister's bed until he was able to bury them in the church, which was to be their refuge for the next eight years.

The Scottish records were also removed from Edinburgh and taken to Stirling Castle, but fell into English hands with Cromwell's capture of the place later in the year. Meanwhile the Scots had patched up at least some of their differences and riposted with another invasion of England which ended in disaster at the battle of Worcester on 3 September 1651. This disaster seemed final. Scotland was obliterated in a manner that went far beyond the ambition of Edward I and his successors to attach Scotland to England as a vassal kingdom. In October 1651 the Commonwealth government declared that England and Scotland were henceforth to be a United

50 *James Gordon of Rothiemay's drawing of Edinburgh Castle, 1647. The drawing conspicuously marks the Spur advanced before the Half-Moon; apart from the main courtyard little is shown on the Rock save the Castle chapel which had replaced St Margaret's.*

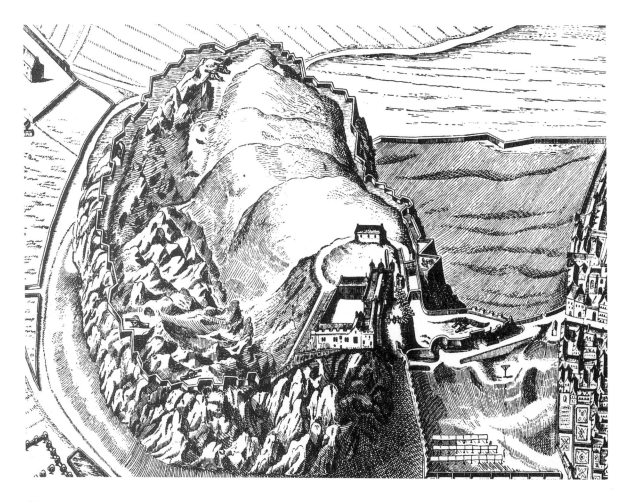

1 Edinburgh from the air: the Castle Rock (centre right), above Princes Street Gardens and (foreground) the rectilinear plan of the 1767 New Town; Arthur's Seat top left.

2 The Castle emerges as a picturesque subject: a view painted by Alexander Nasmyth around 1780.

3   The Castle from Princes Street.

4   *(Right)* The volcanic origins of the Castle Rock. (Prepared by Heather Insh from diagrams by Dr Colin MacFadyen.)

Reconstruction of the Castle Rock volcano illustrating the present-day erosion level.

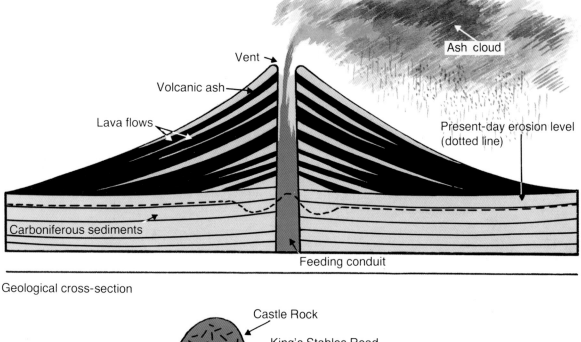

Ash cloud

Vent

Volcanic ash

Lava flows

Present-day erosion level (dotted line)

Carboniferous sediments

Feeding conduit

Geological cross-section

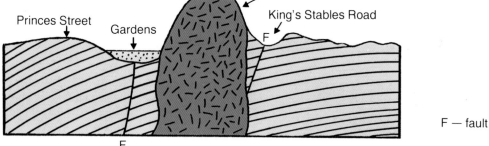

Castle Rock

King's Stables Road

Princes Street

Gardens

F

F — fault

F

Basalt

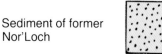

Sediment of former Nor'Loch

Carboniferous sediments

Geological map

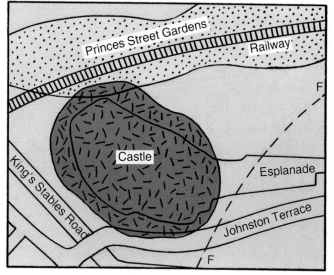

Princes Street Gardens

Railway

F

King's Stables Road

Castle

Esplanade

Johnston Terrace

F

5 The Castle Rock when first seen by Man, about eight thousand years ago: a view from the north. (Painted by Heather Insh from an idea by the author.) The viewpoint is on the ridge now followed by George Street. Beneath the Rock, the bed of the Nor'Loch is today occupied by the railway and part of Princes Street Gardens.

6 Mons Meg: the giant bombard forged at Mons in 1449 and sent as a present to James II, King of Scots, by the Duke of Burgundy, James's uncle by marriage.

7 James IV (1488-1513). In his reign the long drawn out replanning of the Castle was achieved, giving it the new principal courtyard that survives today; the Castle then had a many-sided importance that has not since been surpassed. This portrait, reproduced from James's Book of Hours, shows the King at prayer.

8a The timber roof of the Great Hall. Though the period when the Hall was being built has been a matter of debate, it seems certain that it was completed for James IV at the beginning of the sixteenth century.

8b Two of the stone corbels of Renaissance form supporting the roof, with James IV's cipher (IR4 for *Iacobus Rex quartus*), and the Thistle and the Rose as a symbol of the 1503 marriage of James to the daughter of Henry VII of England.

9 The Crown of Scotland, made in its present form by an Edinburgh
goldsmith for James IV in 1540.

10 The east and north main block of the Palace in Edinburgh Castle, from the Half-Moon Battery. The tower-like structure with its lead-roofed corner turrets and carved panels was raised in 1615-16 above an older building for the 'Homecoming' of James VI of Scotland – who was also, and almost incidentally in this context, James I of England. The two top storeys of the 'tower' seem to have been designed as a Lodging for the King with, above it, a similar Lodging for the Queen. Just seen to the left is the southern part of the Palace, begun about 1500.

11 *(Below)* The defensive lines with domed sentinel boxes built between 1730 and 1737 above the precipices to the north and west of the castle to designs by the military engineer John Romer.

12 *(Above)* A watercolour by Francis Towne dated 13 August 1811 showing Edinburgh Castle on the right and the recently-built Princes Street to the left. Between the two, Princes Street Gardens have not yet been formed.

14 *(Above)* The Glenlivet display of fireworks with music, staged at the Castle and in Princes Street Gardens during the Edinburgh Festival.

13 *(Left)* The Scottish National War Memorial: the Shrine on the very highest point of the Rock with the figure of St Michael.

Commonwealth. The Scottish administration was dismantled and the Scottish Parliament abolished in favour of some representation at Westminster.

Edinburgh Castle, still in a state of disrepair after the 1640 and 1650 sieges, held part of the army of occupation throughout the period of the Commonwealth and Cromwell's Protectorate which followed. Some work was done on the Castle's defences, and this made important changes to the lower parts of the east front. The Spur, which had survived attack, ruin and reconstruction since Ubaldini or one of his fellow-engineers designed it a century earlier, was now done away with. A beginning was made on the great eastern ditch (still extant), and on the low ramparts with batteries rising behind it, the whole designed to provide some measure of flank defence in the mode of contemporary artillery fortification.

This latest English garrison also initiated a lasting shift in the Castle's function. Before Cromwell's army appeared on the scene Scotland had not seen a regular standing force, and as has been observed, a stronghold such as Edinburgh Castle was only 'stuffed with men' in time of international or domestic crisis. As a result accommodation for soldiers was rudimentary or makeshift. A standing garrison needed something better contrived. No contemporary documentary evidence for what was done has been identified, but papers from the reign of Charles II dealing with repairs to the Castle make it clear. To provide the principal barracks, the Great Hall was fitted up with tiers of broad timber galleries round the walls, the galleries being wide enough to hold rows of beds with a walkway next to the open 'well' in the middle of the Great Hall. The Hall was to continue, with many alterations inside and out, for nearly 150 years as the main barrack block in the Castle, and the Cromwellian adaptation may be seen as beginning the long process that reduced the multiple functions of the Castle to the single one of providing for the chief garrison of Scotland. It was probably at the same time that some of the

51 *Oliver Cromwell. During the occupation of the Castle in the 1650s, the Great Hall with lesser places was converted into accommodation for his garrison, beginning a process that was to turn the Castle into a barracks pure and simple.*

vaults under the Great Hall, maybe intended from the time of their construction to accommodate an irregular and intermittent garrison, were set up as barrack rooms that continued in use until the beginning of the nineteenth century, first for soldiers, then for prisoners of war.

The Castle's Commonwealth soldiers belonged to a force which was new in its constitution to Scotland, though many Scots were familiar with similar armies from their service in Europe. Cromwell's New Model Army was a permanent force, with its units disciplined by regulation and with a uniform dress: parade dress was 'a suit of clothes including a red coat faced with blue'. The New Model introduced the colour of the uniforms which was to be of such long standing in the British Army, and some of the first Redcoats in Scotland were quartered in Edinburgh Castle in the 1650s.

The garrison of regular soldiers was continued throughout the period of the Commonwealth, though in its latest years the place had a reduced importance when the English completed a powerful new citadel in Leith about 1658. The Castle's secondary role is the most likely explanation of why the Commonwealth authorities seem at the end to have been rather half-hearted about repairing the siege damage there. The work at Leith contrasted most strongly with the ancient rambling fortress. It was a modern artillery fortification with the angle bastions which, though as noted above, unsuitable for the high rocky perch of Edinburgh Castle, had been the most prominent feature of conventional military engineering in western Europe for a hundred years. The Leith citadel was to be the principal base for the Protectorate military occupation of the east Lowlands.

Last verses of an old song

The Restoration of Charles II in 1660 meant also the restoration of Edinburgh Castle to much of its former status, for Scotland was again a separate realm. The Crown, Sword and Sceptre were returned from their hiding-place in Kinneff Church to their Edinburgh Castle strongroom, and they were used for the opening of Charles's first Parliament on New Year's Day 1661. The national records were sent back from England, and while some were lost at sea on their return voyage, most of those that survived were replaced in James V's Register House between the Palace and the Great Hall. Certain records were, however, now removed to the Laigh (Low) Parliament House, and the transfer from the Castle was eventually completed in 1692.

The damage caused by the bombardments of the previous generation had only partially been made good. In 1662 repairs were carried out to the gun embrasures of the Half-Moon Battery

and elsewhere, but these works were still only provisional, and the precarious state of Charles's Scottish Treasury delayed further operations until 1671. In that year the purse-strings were loosened not only to make a beginning on the ambitious reconstruction of the Palace of Holyrood but also of the Castle, and it is tempting to see the extravagant hand of the Earl (shortly to be created Duke) of Lauderdale influencing the latter, as it certainly influenced the former. At the Castle in 1671–2 a new lower guardhouse was built by the drawbridge, and the roof of the Great Hall repaired; at least some of the windows of the Hall and Palace were fitted with new casement windows, and the rooms of the Royal Apartment in the Palace, last used for a State occasion during Charles I's reign, were painted and their elaborate plaster ceilings whitewashed. The redecoration was carried out for a brief visit by Lauderdale as Commissioner to the 1672 session of Parliament. As Commissioner, the Duke was in effect Viceroy of Scotland for the duration of the Parliament, and while he normally resided in the Royal Apartments at Holyrood, the other palaces including that at the Castle were equally at his disposal. In contrast to this momentary revival of ancient dignity, the repairs to the Great Hall were for the continuation of its recently assumed function as a barracks.

For now Charles II's forces imitated Cromwell's New Model Army not only in the scarlet coats of their uniforms but also in their constitution as a permanent body. A considerable garrison of regular soldiers was to be kept in the Castle from the Restoration until after the First World War. So the Great Hall continued under the new regime with the galleries for beds around the still-open centre of the building, as they had been inserted during the Protectorate.

Under any circumstances of internal or external politics it was necessary to attend to the most important place of strength in the country, but there were also immediate threats within Scotland from the militant Covenanters, who posed an intractable problem to Charles II's Scottish government. A determined group resisting the church settlement made after the Restoration had already risen in rebellion in 1666. In the next decade the breakdown of Lauderdale's attempts to reach a compromise led to tension. This in turn must have helped general proposals for the Castle by the military engineer Captain John Slezer in 1674, and the next building campaign there between 1677 and 1680. In 1678, while work was in progress, there were alarming reports of a plan by the dissidents to execute a *coup* by seizing the Castle, and a second Covenanting rebellion did in fact break out during the following year.

From 1677 Slezer improved and remodelled several parts of the fortifications. Along the circuit of the western defences the ground was levelled and graded 'for the Rounds [sentries on patrol] to go along in the night time, it being at

present impossible to do it on a stormy night'. The lower works of the east front were the subject of a lot of thought but limited action. Here eventually the ditch begun in Cromwell's time was taken forward, thus setting out the basic plan of the defences that existed until the 1880s and, as far as the ditch is concerned, still survives. Within the Castle there were new works for the internal perimeter of the west side of the citadel (52), and parts of these, loopholed for artillery and muskets, are the only works of the reign of Charles II to remain more or less intact today. The gate that pierces the defensive wall, enigmatically called Foog's Gate, has the site but probably not the form of the original; below it there was an elaborate loopholed outwork for 'close fight', identified during the 1988–91 excavations.

Also inside the Castle, besides general repairs to a number of buildings, Slezer constructed a new main guardhouse and, also new, a magazine in the north-west part of the Rock, which held 406 barrels of gunpowder in 1679. The comfort of the soldiers in the Great Hall barracks was attended to by renewing their bedding, and by building a malt barn and malt kiln for a new

52 *'The New Retrenchment within the Castle of Edinburgh' by John Slezer. It shows the new Charles II defences with the broken Mons Meg dumped in the foreground.*

brewhouse. There were funds for some ornament too, with new wooden lofts decorated with the Doric order in the sixteenth-century Chapel.

The renovated Castle was visited in November 1679 by the King's brother, James Duke of Albany and York (the former was his Scottish and the latter his English title, just as later he succeeded to the thrones as James VII of Scotland and II of England). Though disguised as a State visit, James's first stay in Scotland was in fact an enforced temporary exile to quieten agitation against him in England as the Roman Catholic heir to the throne. The Catholic prince made quite a success of his stay in Calvinist Scotland, and he revisited the Castle in 1681 as Commissioner to Charles II's third and last Scottish Parliament. When James was in Edinburgh Mons Meg was brought into service for what proved to be the last time to join in a salute. The ancient bombard burst on discharge – the fracture of its iron hoops near the chamber is still conspicuous – and the gun which had belonged to eight generations of Scottish monarchs was unceremoniously dumped near the road leading up from the Portcullis Gate (see **52**).

James did not come to Scotland during his reign as James VII and II. In his northern realm he enjoyed the traditional loyalty of the majority of people in spite of the insensitivity of setting up Catholic institutions and organs of propaganda in Edinburgh soon after his accession in 1685. James's term of power in England ended in 1688, when his son-in-law William of Orange landed in Devon on 5 November and James fled to France. William and Mary were proclaimed joint sovereigns of England on 13 February 1689, but how this English action was to affect Scotland remained unclear for the next five months. The Catholic Duke of Gordon, appointed as Governor of the Castle by James VII and one of his firmest supporters, began to make the place ready to defend itself. The preparation was rather hesitant, for part of the garrison of under two hundred was disaffected, there was a shortage of ammunition and provisions, and in the confused situation the Duke thought his services might be more useful elsewhere.

In the crisis of state that confronted Scotland, a Convention of Estates, a traditional 'reduced' form of the Scottish Parliament, met under the Commissionership of the Duke of Hamilton. Since the Convention had not been commanded by the King – could not have been, as he was in France – there was clearly some question as to the legitimacy of the body, in which strong elements inclined towards the settlement of the succession on William and Mary. The Convention ordered the picketing of the Castle on 18 March. On the following day John Grahame of Claverhouse, recently created Viscount Dundee, left the Convention to confer with Gordon at the west postern of the Castle, and rode off to raise a force to fight for King James. A four-months' civil war began.

On 25 March Major-General Mackay took command of the siege of the Castle and opened the attack on it (**53**). The Convention, declaring that James VII had forfeited the Scottish Crown, offered it to William and Mary who accepted it on 11 May 1689. At the siege, the Duke of Gordon's counter-battery fire to the east was inhibited by fear of the damage it might cause to the town. There was an acute shortage of food and water, some of the Castle's garrison deserted and sickness broke out. The documentary record of an epidemic was strikingly amplified during the 1988–91 excavations, when a cemetery datable to three centuries before was discovered (**54**). None of the young men whose skeletons were found in it had suffered wounds, and all by inference had died of disease. The Castle surrendered on 13 June and the garrison marched out on the next day. Any immediate hope of retrieving King James's Scottish cause on the battlefield ended with Viscount Dundee's death at Killiecrankie in July.

53 The 'Long Siege' of 1689, when the Duke of Gordon held the Castle for James VII and II: a reconstruction drawing of the fighting platform of the Half-Moon. (Drawing by David Simon.)

54 *Skeletons in the makeshift cemetery near the western entry of the Castle, probably members of the garrison who died of disease during the 1689 siege; a photograph from the 1988—91 archaeological excavations.*

Meanwhile James had landed in Ireland and the war continued there. In Scotland substantial disaffection continued (most sharply remembered today for the massacre at Glencoe in 1692) and the word 'Jacobite' was coined to describe supporters of the old regime. William and Mary's government in Scotland certainly did not feel secure, and in the capital it proceeded between 1689 and 1695 to repair siege damage to the Castle. The ramparts had suffered considerably, especially the walls and parapet of the Half-Moon Battery and the Forewall, there was a large breach at the west postern, part of the magazine and main guardhouse built in Charles II's time by John Slezer had been destroyed, and the Chapel had been hit. While this work was being done, normal maintenance repairs were being carried on at the Munition House and the roof of the Great-Hall-cum-barracks. Of these operations there are alone recognizable today the parapets of the Half-Moon (55) and the Forewall, both still unchanged from their late seventeenth-century state.

King William II, to give him his Scottish title, did not visit Scotland, and probably like Charles II had no intention of doing so; nor did William's widow Mary nor her successor Queen Anne. It was in Anne's reign that there came about at last a complete political union between Scotland

55 *The parapet of the Half-Moon, rebuilt in this form after the siege of 1689.*

and England, with the abolition of a separate Scottish administration and Parliament. On 19 March 1707, accompanied by a salute from the guns of the Castle, the Act of Union was read to the Scottish Parliament and ordered to be recorded. 'Now, there's an end of an old song', Chancellor Seafield is reported to have exclaimed, giving the Act with his signature to the Clerk. When Parliament rose, the Crown, Sword and Sceptre were taken back to the Castle from Parliament House and replaced in their vault within the Palace there.

Until that date these Crown Jewels had continued their ancient function as symbols of the authority of the Parliament and its Commissioner representing the person of the monarch.

They were treated with a deep if rather casual affection, quite unlike the high-security reverence of today. The Crown might be given to visitors to hold, and in 1692 someone had dropped it, breaking off the orb and cross (the rather crude repair, one of several, is still visible). Now a sad farewell speech was written for the Crown:

> I royal diadem relinquished stand
> By all my friends and robbèd of my land
> So left bereft of all I did command . . .

The openings of the vault were blocked up with masonry. In time people wondered whether the Honours of Scotland really survived there.

CHAPTER FIVE

North Britain

The United Kingdom

Louis XIV of France, for mixed reasons of history and interest, supported the cause of the Stuarts and gave sanctuary to them in exile. In 1707 his advisers, optimistically reading intelligence reports, suggested that opposition in Scotland to the Union from the Presbyterian Whigs, as well as the Jacobites, was very strong. It was felt that a French-supported attempt could place James Francis Edward Stuart, son of James VII and II, on a re-established Scottish throne as James VIII – and maybe afterwards on the throne of England as well. On 23 March 1708 a French naval squadron appeared in the Firth of Forth: on board were six thousand of Louis's soldiers and James (56). The fleet missed an opportunity to make a landing, and was then intercepted and turned back. For Queen Anne's United Kingdom government in London the incident raised a frightening ghost of the ancient Franco-Scottish alliance.

The Scottish noblemen and lairds supposed to have plotted with the would-be invaders, including the Duke of Gordon, the Earls of Moray and Seaforth, the Lords Belhaven and Traquair, were confined in Edinburgh Castle. The House of Commons desired that Edinburgh and Stirling castles, together with the Highland outpost of Fort William, should be strengthened as soon as possible. Work began at the three places on 1 July 1708, directed after some very hasty planning by Captain Theodore Dury. After the

Union, Dury was still engineer for Scotland, but he was now under the control of the Board of Ordnance in London as the body responsible for work at all military establishments in the United Kingdom. Dury's programme for Edinburgh Castle took in four main elements: a more satisfactory adaptation of the Great Hall as a barracks; a new building to house some of the garrison officers as well as the minister (or chaplain) and the gunners; improvements to several parts of the perimeter defences; and a massive new fortification for the eastern defences, called in the contemporary jargon of military engineering a 'hornwork' from the horn-shaped projections at each end of its front. At Edinburgh this was mysteriously christened 'le grand sécret'.

For some unknown reason the Great Hall scheme was not proceeded with (and it was not to be converted into proper quarters until 1737). The officers' block went ahead as a twin-range unit on the west side of the principal courtyard, notable as the first large structure in the Castle purpose-built as garrison accommodation. The 'big secret' ran into difficulties. The Board of Ordnance's first intervention in Scotland was to send one of its engineers, Captain O'Bryen, to report on Dury's proposals. O'Bryen arrived with operations under way, was alarmed by what he saw, continued the work with his own alterations and reported to the Board with a revised design. All work on the Edinburgh defences was suspended in March 1710 while the

56 *In 1708 a French fleet in the Firth of Forth intends to land: Louis XIV's attempt to put the Stuarts back on the throne.*

Board's Second Engineer (or deputy chief) Talbot Edwards journeyed to Scotland and made a further report. With several choices for the east front, some of them very costly, the Board was unable to make up its mind on what to do or how much to spend. After another false start the beginnings of the hornwork were eventually abandoned incomplete. Theodore Dury's more modest improvements to the fortifications proceeded, however, and two new five-gun batteries called Dury's Battery and Butts Battery were completed in 1713 (57). The first-named reinforced the armament to the south. The second held the principal armament of the Castle towards the west, together with a further emplacement at a higher level on the site called Hawk Hill – now obscured by the huge mass of

the late eighteenth-century New Barracks. Dury's Battery and Butts Battery survive, together with the north flanker for the hornwork. So does the block for the garrison officers and others, today called the Queen Anne Building.

The episode of the hornwork heralded a substantial change in the fortunes of what had been regarded as the premier fortress of Scotland. In terms of engineering, the case against Dury's idea was that, built out with conspicuous prominence on the Castle Hill, *le grand sécret* would have been unanswerably vulnerable to attacking fire on its flanks. And while the design might have been improved, there was a more fundamental engineering argument against major works. Edinburgh Castle's natural defences were very strong, but this same quality meant that the site did not accommodate itself to a modern system of fortification. Alongside such points of military science, the Act of Union was emerging as a new and substantial factor. Before 1707, the Castle had been the chief fortress and arsenal, and to a degree the treasury of a separate country. Now that Scotland had become North Britain, the Castle no longer had the same need for the powerful defences that had been taken for granted during the centuries of its political eminence. Great Britain's arsenal was now the Tower of London. What had been the chief treasures of the Castle, the Honours, no longer had any importance as symbols of the monarch. The place henceforth certainly had to be fully defensible, but the fortifications did not so

imperatively need be on the scale of earlier times. The choices before the Board of Ordnance make the point: whether the defences of the Castle should be capable of resisting a 'siege royal' (that is, with a full train of artillery); or siege by a still potent but lesser train; or simply be capable of resisting 'insult' or surprise by a small force. In earlier years, the question that there was any choice would not have arisen.

The Board did not fully implement any scheme during Queen Anne's reign, and more comprehensive improvements to the defences at a middling level were not to be attempted until the 1730s. Anne's government, however, made concessions to its opponents that reduced the immediate threat of insurrection and a lull followed, to end in a new crisis when the Elector of Hanover succeeded to the throne of the United Kingdom as George I after Anne's death in 1714.

57 *The battery of 1708–13 to reinforce the armament to the south of the Castle, called after its designer 'Dury's Battery'. The building was erected in 1708–13 to accommodate officers of the garrison, the minister, the Castle gunners, and others, and is known today as the Queen Anne Building above what is probably the lower structure of the late fifteenth-century Gunhouse.*

In the rising of 1715 the Jacobites made an attempt on the Castle. The place was not perhaps seriously endangered, although one of the investing parties in a surprise move broke in at the west postern, and another blew up lengths of Dury's ill-starred *grand sécret* (its surviving fragments, visible in Princes Street Gardens well below the level of the Esplanade, still give some impression of its intended large scale).

The Castle was subsequently used to confine prisoners taken during the rising, while the authorities concentrated their attention on improving security in the Highlands. The general situation continued to be highly disturbing to the Hanoverian government with some cause, for after the outbreak of war between Spain and Great Britain in 1718, a small Spanish force landed in the West Highlands during the following year. The invaders were joined by some Jacobite Highlanders, but were defeated in Glenshiel by the Commander-in-Chief in Scotland, Lieutenant-General George Carpenter, marching from Edinburgh Castle.

The incident prompted a survey of accommodation in the Castle which provides a detailed picture of the use of its buildings: around the principal courtyard, the Great Hall retains its rudimentary Cromwellian arrangements as a soldiers' barracks, and opposite it is James V's Munition House still in use for ordnance stores. On the west side, the new block is coming into use with apartments for the Barrack Master and Gunner, the Fort Major and subaltern officers, the Serjeant of the Castle, the minister and the schoolmaster, though several rooms are still empty. To the east, the Palace is in a state of transition. Part is empty, and part has fairly lowly uses. Half of the Laigh Hall is the barrack master's store, the little birth room of James VI and the Inner Chamber next to it are designated 'Drinking Rooms or Sutlers Apartment' (almost all of the Palace cellarage has been converted to beer stores). On a higher social plane, the Governor has most of the south-east corner of the building as his Apartment. The 1615–16 tower rising at the north end of the Palace, which

58 *A contemporary sketch of the Jacobite attempt to surprise Edinburgh Castle in 1715 by breaking in at the western sallyport.*

has been identified as containing the private Royal Lodgings, is still named as the King's Apartment, and the king also has three rooms at ground level, including the southern half of the Laigh Hall. Here in the 1719 survey is the last known mention of accommodation designated for royalty in the Castle. In the future everything in the stronghold is to be turned over to the military.

Lawlessness and disaffection in the Highlands continued in spite of the check the Jacobite cause had received at Glenshiel, and the whole Hanoverian position north of the Border seemed insecure. In July 1724 Major-General George Wade was ordered to proceed to Scotland to investigate and propose remedies (**59**). Wade's

59 *George Wade, then a major-general, was
appointed Commander-in-Chief in North Britain in
1724. During his period of office – best known for
the construction of the first military roads in the
Highlands – he pressed successfully for
improvements to the defences of Edinburgh Castle.*

initial report was soon followed by his appointment as 'Commander-in-chief of all His Majesty's forces, castles, forts and barracks, in 'North Britain', and also by further recommendations by him from April 1725. While Wade's first concern was with the Highlands, in the construction of forts and the first strategic roads there, he also successfully urged the need for works on the fortifications and buildings of Edinburgh Castle (and to a lesser degree at Dumbarton Castle). Immediate repairs were made to the most vulnerable parts of the defences. Then, between 1730 and 1737, the whole of the northern and western perimeter was rebuilt to designs by the Board of Ordnance engineer for North Britain, Captain John Romer.

The work, like the rest of the masonry construction in the Castle at the time, was executed by William Adam as Master Mason to the Board of Ordnance. The angled lengths of wall and domed sentinel boxes above the precipices have been one of the most dramatic elements in the prospect of the Castle ever since (60). In addition, the masonry of the main ditch formed during the Cromwellian occupation was at last completed in 1742. The improvements had the objective of protecting the Castle from surprise, and defending it against an investment with limited artillery support. No attempt was made to give the Castle the capability to withstand modern full-scale siege, so abiding by the eventual decision of the Board of Ordnance in Queen Anne's reign not to proceed with any

60 *A sentinel box on the western defences, built in the 1730s by William Adam to a design by the military engineer John Romer.*

work comparable in scale to Dury's abandoned forework. To the reasons that applied then there had been added a new one, for the focus of military attention had moved to the Highlands with Fort George (the first of the name) at Inverness, and Fort Augustus, built by the Board on Wade's recommendation.

Within the Castle, in 1737 the interior of the Great Hall was altered to a more conventional layout giving beds for 310 men in six large barrack rooms. There were three floors, the uppermost intruding into the James IV hammer-beam roof and effectively hiding it from casual inspection. And in 1742 a new building was raised towards the north-west of the Rock (replacing the Main Guard House of the reign of Charles II) with its main block as the Governor's House, and wings for the Master Gunner and the

61 The building known as the Governor's House, erected in 1740–2 to a design by Dugal Campbell. It was in fact three separate houses: the central block for the Governor, and wings for the Master Gunner and the Store-Keeper.

Storekeeper. It is an outstanding example of Board of Ordnance design, with heavy stepped gables rising from channelled pilasters, its porch with a triangular pediment. (The Governor kept this official residence until 1860 when the governorship lapsed; after the revival of the office in 1935 the Governor has had part of the north wing, with the remainder used as the Officers' Mess.) The Governor's House, by Dugal Campbell, is the most distinguished among the Georgian military buildings of the Castle (**61**).

Wade's next-but-one successor as Commander-in-Chief was General George Cope, who marched out of the Castle in the autumn of 1745 to intercept Prince Charles Edward, turned back in the mountains of Badenoch, embarked at Inverness to return to the Lowlands and to encounter defeat at Prestonpans. The Jacobite army occupying Edinburgh in September and October 1745 picketed the Castle, though it lacked artillery to mount an active siege. The Redcoat commander General Preston fired on the town, inducing the citizens to petition the Prince to raise the blockade. Charles Edward consented soon before he set out on the march that took him to Derby. After this inconclusive episode, the Castle was not to be in contact with war again.

Georgian garrison and prison of war

Many of the Jacobite prisoners taken in 1745 and 1746 were lodged in the Castle. Some of them, such as the 170 or so recruits captured at sea, were there for only a short time. After the defeat of Prince Charles Edward at Culloden others, who included the Earl of Kellie, Glengarry, McDonald of Glencoe and McDonald of Kingsburgh, were confined for longer periods, and the pressure strained the Castle's resources of reasonably secure places. The detention space in the guardhouses at the main drawbridge and the western sallyport, together with the 'black hole' (presumably the ancient sheriff's prison in the sub-vaults under the Great Hall, by then normally only used as punishment cells for soldiers) were all pressed into service. Jacobite suspects were still being brought in as late as 1753. They were not the only inmates in custody, for although the Scottish Privy Council had ordained as long ago as 1607 that only civil prisoners guilty of treason and other great offences should be confined in the Castle – the burgh tolbooth was supposed to look after the rest – the Castle was still being used as a common gaol in the middle of the eighteenth century. The Lieutenant Governor of 1752, Richard Coren,

complained that in consequence officers had to sleep two in a room to make room for prisoners.

The alarm caused to the government by the 1745 rising was most urgently expressed in new Highland fortifications, notably in the construction of the second Fort George east of Inverness by William Skinner, Chief Engineer in North Britain, and in a much extended network of military roads. There were to be no new defences raised at Edinburgh Castle though considerable improvements were planned on paper. Immediate new building there was confined to a large cart shed at Mills Mount. It is rather remarkable that this basic structure, run up in great haste to

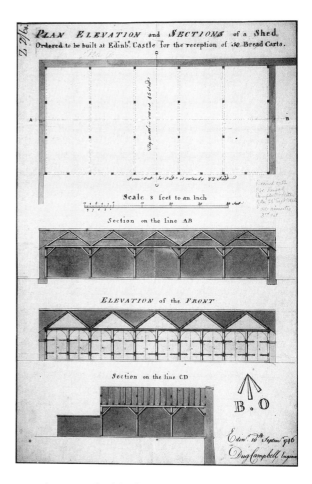

62 *The Cart Shed built on Mills Mount in 1746 immediately after the Jacobite rising. Subsequently converted into a barracks, it now forms part of the Castle restaurant (see also 1).*

meet a temporary need, has survived in recognizable form to the present day, after adaptation as
barracks, tea-room, shop and now restaurant
(**62**).

A programme was drawn up by Skinner to
improve provision for men and munitions. In
1748–54 the main powder magazine in the north-
west part of the Rock, dating from the time of
Charles II, was pulled down and replaced near
the same site by another of improved design,

63 *A mid-eighteenth-century view of the Castle
from the east, showing the defences towards the
Castle Hill which survived in this form until the
1880s.*

flanked on each side by large Ordnance Storehouses to form a courtyard. The ground floors of
both of the storehouses towards the court were
arcaded, and the screen wall closing the court
was provided with stone sentry boxes (which,
with their positions moved, survive). The rear of

97

the magazine and storehouse group was extremely plain; and it was to be condemned for its ugliness in the next century (**64**). The arms and equipment were then taken from James V's Munition House while, as part of a general tidying-up operation, Mons Meg was sent with other unserviceable guns and material to the Tower of London.

As far as soldiers' accommodation was concerned, in 1755 the vacated Munition House, once St Mary's Church, was demolished and replaced by a new barrack block. The latter, on the north side of the principal courtyard, was called the North Barracks (completely refashioned, it has been since the 1920s the Scottish National War Memorial), while the Great Hall opposite was called the South Barracks. Now all four sides of the courtyard were exclusively used by the army. As well as the barracks to north and south, there was to the west the Queen Anne block with apartments for officers and office-bearers and accommodation for the gunners. The Palace, on the east of the courtyard, now lost almost all reminders of royal use. The Board of Ordnance survey of 1719 had still noted some rooms there as the king's, though they had not been used by royalty since the reign of Charles I. The next survey, made in 1754, has no such designations. The 1615–16 Royal Lodgings have become rooms for subaltern officers, and the

64 *The 1748 Magazine flanked by the 1753–4 twin Ordnance Stores; a view of their austere appearance from the west (the photograph is of about 1850 – it also shows Mills Mount Cart Shed extended as barracks, left; and the New Barracks, right).*

65 *For more than half a century after 1757 the vaults under the Great Hall and the Queen Anne building were used as a prison of war. The prisoners have left a large number of graffiti, one of the best being a very simple political cartoon carved by a Frenchman captured during the American War of Independence. It shows the prime minister of Great Britain Lord North – who bore a fair degree of responsibility for the conflict – hanging from a gallows with the Anglo-French rhyming caption* 'LORD NORD 1780'.

whole of the Laigh Hall is now a small-arms store.

The only concession to the royal past in the survey, and a rather unexpected touch of sentiment, is a note marking 'The Closet wherein King James ye 1st was born'. Other changes to the use of rooms flowed from the occupation by the Governor – who had previously had an apartment in the Palace – of his residence built in 1742. Indeed the changes just noticed, which amount to a substantial shift from the past, may have their origins in thinking that was going on before the 'Forty-Five.

The new dispositions reduced the demands on the ranges of vaults beneath the level of the courtyard as soldiers' quarters. The best-remembered functions of these vaults began soon afterwards, during the Seven Years' War against France (1756–63). In April 1757 HMS Solebay captured a French privateer off the east coast and brought the ship and 78 crewmen to Leith. The sailors were put in the Castle. From this accidental beginning developed a frequent practice. There were several escapes, for the improvised arrangements were far from secure. By the end of the war there were 500 Frenchmen in the Castle, to be escorted to Leith and repatriated. The Castle again became a prison of war during the American War of Independence. Between 1778 and 1782 about 990 prisoners of war of five nationalities – American, French, Spanish, Dutch and Irish – passed through the Castle.

In these decades of the eighteenth century, developments of a different kind emerged. The Castle Hill has been seen in the grim context of a place of execution; in time it won a more cheerful reputation as a lovers' walk, and also as a promenade for citizens taking staider exercise. In 1753 the convex ridge of the hill was made up with spoil from the site-preparation of the burgh's Exchange – now the City Chambers – to form a parade ground. The work improved its amenity as a place to take the air, and so the Castle was brought more into public awareness as a striking part of Edinburgh's ambience.

Linked to this awareness, appreciation of the Castle as an illustration of the Picturesque was also becoming apparent over the same span of years. The powerful forms of the stronghold from the east, the Half-Moon Battery with the Palace above the crags, had clear potential as a subject for painting. Its possibilities were explored by Paul Sandby, a figure who moved easily between military and artistic concerns: Sandby came to Scotland to assist in the post-Culloden military survey of the Highlands, but as an aspect of his increasing involvement with topographical art he made studies of the Castle amongst other places. Perhaps the most memorable transfiguration of the stronghold into a work of art, however, is a picture of about 1780 by Alexander Nasmyth who, in a manner characteristic of the *genre*, reshapes the scenery to give maximum impact to a Castle whose harsher realities of military building are softened. The painting is very much in the tradition of Claude Lorrain, for in addition to the supremely picturesque drama of its site, the Castle's buildings displayed the contrast of round and rectilinear forms that was one of Claude's favoured conventions (**colour plate 2**).

The period of the Seven Years' War and the American War of Independence had seen no significant building activity. The next conflict, the war with revolutionary France, caused a huge expansion of the army and a flurry of barrack construction throughout Britain. Between 1796 and 1799 the largest structure in the Castle was raised: the New Barracks for 600 men and their officers, together with specialized accommodation such as prison rooms replacing more primitive locations. The New Barracks were contrived on the last feasible large and comparatively open space within the perimeter, the awkwardly rising site in the south-west quarter of the Rock between Hawk Hill and Butts Battery – and even here some earlier remains had to be removed. The block, perhaps designed by Thomas Rudyerd, is an interestingly contrived building of six storeys (**66**). In its east elevation towards the interior of the Castle its height is disguised, for the lower three storeys lie below the level of the cobbled courtyard that fronts the building. From this side a structure of three storeys is visible, its ends and pedimented centre (all with Roman Doric porches) advanced, and with a balustraded terrace on great arches giving access to the porch at the north end (**67**). This complicated adjustment to the site makes the composition of the principal elevation far from easy to take in at first sight. By contrast the west elevation, set back from the perimeter defences above the rocky slopes, is straightforward and in its plainness overwhelming in scale. As built, a big open arcade ran along the full length of the barracks above a lowest level of simple windows, and below four upper levels of similar openings. Although in the future this Georgian colossus was to be thought of as one of the ugliest elements in the Castle, and there were

66 The New Barracks was built in 1796–9 to meet the needs of the swollen garrison during the wars with revolutionary and Napoleonic France, and has since dominated the view of the Castle from the west. The verandah was added in 1893.

67 *The principal elevation of the New Barracks, from the east.*

to be a number of schemes drastically to alter it, it remains as conceived save for the addition of an iron verandah closing off the arcade, put up in 1893.

With this major addition of soldiers' accommodation, the South Barracks in the Great Hall could then be converted into a military hospital, causing more alteration inside and outside. The clutter of lesser army buildings expanded during the period up to the battle of Waterloo in 1815, so that virtually the whole of the Rock was now developed. The French wars also saw the climax of the Castle's use as prison of war. Again most of the captives were sailors, who began to arrive from 1796, but soldiers were later brought in from Wellington's victories in Spain.

The prison was fitted out piecemeal with massive ironwork in an endeavour to make it more secure, and in general it was better organized than hitherto, taking in a small palisaded exercise yard. Although there was an establishment of warding staff as well as soldiers on guard, serious problems of security remained. These were emphasized by a mass escape in April 1811 when 49 prisoners cut a hole in the Castle wall and lowered themselves on ropes down the precipitous south crags. By this date specially designed depots for prisoners of war were being built throughout Britain (the largest in Scotland was on the site of today's Perth Prison), and the escape helped towards a decision to abandon the Castle for this function. It was not closed down altogether, continuing with a very much reduced number of captives, and used as a punishment centre for men from the depots.

During the French Revolutionary and Napoleonic wars the Castle had, as on earlier occasions, contained an extremely mixed body of men, taking in Frenchmen, Spaniards, Dutchmen, Danes, Germans, Italians and Americans;

with international feuds developing particularly between the French and their reluctant Spanish allies. Most of the prisoners, however, employed their enforced leisure peacefully to produce articles for sale to visitors – a fine ship model is preserved in the Scottish United Services Museum in the Castle – and to forge banknotes for more stealthy distribution.

Symbols of a High Romance

'Scott's house in Edinburgh is divinely situated' Coleridge remarked during his 1803 tour with

68 *The eighteenth century contributed a greater volume of new construction than any other period and most of its fortifications and buildings survive, either more or less as built or as later altered. The key runs clockwise from bottom centre of the*

drawing. Of the fortifications, Dury's Battery (1) and Butts Battery (2), both of 1708–13, have been altered, but from there on they are as built or nearly so: the 1730–7 perimeter above the crags (3) round to the flanking defence (4) for the ill-fated advanced work, le grand sécret, of 1708 – to the east is the still-visible fragment of the latter – up to the point of junction with the Portcullis Gate (5). Of the buildings, the 1755 North Barracks (6 – the Great Hall was the South Barracks) was transformed as the Scottish National War Memorial; the 1708–13 Queen Anne Building (7) was internally gutted as the military museum that became the Scottish United Services Museum; the 1796–9 New Barracks (8) and the 1742 Governor's House (9) are both not much altered; though the 1753–4 Ordnance Stores (10) were baronialized as a military hospital which is now all to be the Scottish United Services Museum; while the 1746 Cart Shed (11) on Mills Mount was turned into a barracks and is now part of the Castle restaurant.

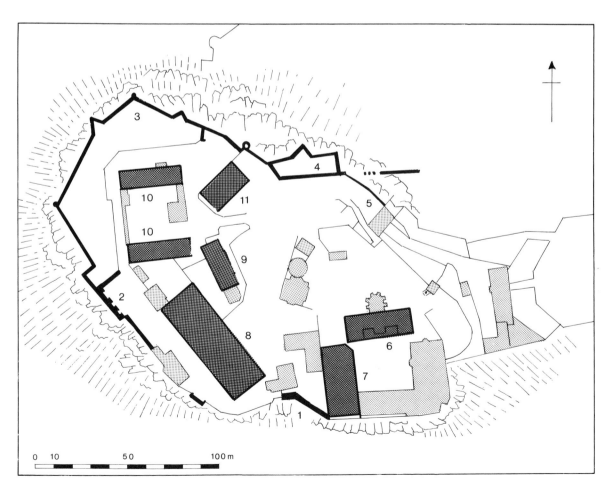

the Wordsworths, 'it looks up a street full upon the rock and castle'. A generation of romantics was perceiving the stronghold with an increased and more general sense of aesthetic appreciation than before, an appreciation helped by further developments bringing the Castle much more into prominence. The contours of the Castle Hill, made regular in 1753, were developed between 1816 and 1820 to make the Esplanade of today; it was widened, its sides were built up in stone, and it was ornamented with turrets to the south. In addition a more fundamental enlargement of the view of the Castle had been going on from 1767, when James Craig's plan for a New Town was approved, and the fashionable streets and squares from Princes Street northward were constructed during the rest of the century. The Castle was brought right into the townscape of Edinburgh as the climax of an unparalleled vista, which was emphasized after 1816, when an Act of Parliament was obtained for private gardens to be laid out between Princes Street and the Castle. Major work on them started in 1821–2, when the Nor' Loch was drained. Walter Scott lived just off Princes Street at No. 9 North Castle Street (now 39 Castle Street) from 1802 until 1826, enjoying prospects of the fortress on the northern face of the crags from the bow windows of the house.

These developments coincided with the beginning of the new romantic interest in Scotland's past so much furthered by Scott. He played a leading part in the first concrete display of concern with the ancient glories of the Castle: the recovery of the Honours of Scotland – the Crown, Sword and Sceptre – from the obscurity of the vault where they had been walled up in 1707 (69). On 4 February 1818, authorized by a warrant from the Prince Regent, the Scottish Officers of State and Walter Scott entered the vault when the masonry blocking had been cut away. The party watched as the great iron-bound chest was broken open, for its keys had long ago disappeared. Everyone was aware of the long-standing suspicion that the chest might be empty. In Scott's words:

The chest seemed to return a hollow and empty sound to the strokes of the hammer, and even those whose expectations had been most sanguine felt at the moment the probability of disappointment, and could not but be sensible that, should the result of the search confirm these forebodings, it would only serve to show that a national affront and injury had been sustained, for which it might be difficult, or rather impossible to obtain any redress. The joy was therefore extreme when, the ponderous lid of the chest being forced open, at the expense of some time and labour, the Regalia were discovered lying at the bottom covered with linen cloths, exactly as they had been left in the year 1707 ... The rejoicing was so genuine and sincere as plainly to show that, however altered in other respects, the people of Scotland had lost nothing of that national enthusiasm which formerly had displayed itself in grief for the loss of these emblematic Honours, and now was expressed in joy for their recovery.

The Regalia were ceremonially viewed by George IV on the occasion of his visit to Scotland in 1822, a visit which Sir Walter Scott (created baronet in 1820) had helped to promote; the King going in grand procession (70) to the Castle on 22 August, during that fortnight which did a great deal to form new images of North Britain. The Crown, Sword and Sceptre had been retained in the vault designed to hold them in security two hundred years before, and soon after their rediscovery had been put on view to the general public for a normal admittance charge of one shilling, under the surveillance of a specially appointed keeper (71).

The fifteenth-century bombard Mons Meg was the subject of the next reintroduction to the Scottish public's eye. After it was taken to the

69 (Above right) *The Regalia, the Honours of Scotland, are rediscovered on 4 February 1818 in the vault where they had been entombed since the Act of Union, with Walter Scott among those of the official party: a sketch by Sir David Wilkie.*

70 (Below right) *The procession of George IV to the Castle on 22 August 1822, seen from the Half-Moon Battery.*

71 *A notice in the* Edinburgh Evening Courant, *24 May 1819: one shilling is charged to view the Honours of Scotland in the Castle.*

Tower of London in 1754, the great gun had become so popular that prolonged lobbying was necessary to persuade the Armouries to relinquish it. Scott took part in applying pressure, but on this occasion he was only a figurehead, for the prime mover was the Society of Antiquaries of Scotland. At last agreement was reached that Mons should be returned to Scotland. An ornate cast-iron carriage bearing the traditional history and battle honours of the gun was made by the Royal Carriage Department, and Mons with her new mounting was shipped to Leith (72). After some further delay the Society of Antiquaries fixed on 9 March 1829 'for the removal of this venerable relic of antiquity from the Naval Yard at Leith to the Castle of Edinburgh,' and Mons was escorted there by three troops of cavalry and

72 *Mons Meg mounted on the cast-iron carriage made by the Royal Carriage Department for her return from the Tower of London in 1829.*

a regiment of foot, to be emplaced for the next century and a half on the disused mortar battery towards the Forth, overlooking the New Town.

When the huge weapon was being piped into position no one knew that she was being set down just outside St Margaret's Chapel, for Scott and his contemporaries were unaware that the Chapel still existed. This, the most ancient building in the Castle, located in an area that had developed more than three centuries before as one of the main centres of the arsenal, had been completely lost to mind and sight in alterations and additions. At an unknown date in the sixteenth century it had been replaced by a new chapel attached to the east gable of the earlier building. The replacement, subsequently the garrison chapel, remodelled several times and ending with a Gothic revival façade, was still being used in 1829. The old St Margaret's, out of ecclesiastical use, was converted to a magazine. By 1829 it was the storehouse of the Master Gunner, and his yard was adjacent to it. The outer walls had been raised in height, new openings cut through them and the roof obscured. The case of the Chapel underlines the fact that the stronghold was still discharging all the functions of the chief station of the British forces in Scotland.

The dominance of military considerations, however, was just beginning to ebb, and for several decades there was an alternation between the further retrieval, or sometimes invention, of past glory, and the satisfaction of the garrison's needs. On the one hand, in 1836 the so-called 'Queen Mary's rooms', the ancient Inner Chamber in the Palace and the adjoining Cabinet where James VI and I was born, were vacated by the army and kept exclusively for exhibition to the public. On the other, the first Victorian building constructed was a small prison, of 1840–2, for exclusive military use – all use of the Castle for civil prisoners was now discontinued – near the New Barracks where the garrison's prison rooms were then located. Influenced by the latest wave of reform ideas for civil jails, the Army decided to build its new

detached prison in the Castle, distinct from the garrison's normal requirements, to take in soldiers brought from stations throughout Scotland. At the time the perfect regime for civilian prisoners was seen as solitary confinement with labour, provided for in the latest model prisons at Perth and Pentonville. The design for the Castle was a miniature version of these, with an open 'hall' giving access to two floors of cells (73). Each solitary cell was centrally heated by a warm-air system, and each had a wooden bed and shelves. The prison, extended later in the nineteenth century, was last used in 1923 just after the withdrawal of the garrison to Redford Barracks in the Edinburgh suburbs.

The keen interest of Daniel Wilson – archaeologist, secretary of the Society of Antiquaries of Scotland and subsequently educational reformer in Canada – in the vestiges of history in the Castle was rewarded in 1845 when he recognized St Margaret's Chapel hidden by centuries of change. The Society of Antiquaries again took the lead in persuading the authorities to undertake the first, and as it turned out the most conservative, of a series of Victorian enterprises intended to make the structures of the Castle more in keeping with their spectacular setting. The rediscovered Chapel was looked on with a special romantic reverence, for since the later Middle Ages it had been thought to be the very shrine where Queen Margaret had worshipped. (Daniel Wilson himself soon recognized, however, as we ourselves recognize, that from its style it cannot be so early.) A modest restoration in 1851–2 by Lieutenant-Colonel George Phillpotts, the Commanding Royal Engineer for Scotland, and Maximilian Grant added a new neo-Romanesque doorpiece and took in the demolition of later accretions including the garrison chapel. It was soon afterwards proposed that the little building might be used by the Episcopal chaplain to the garrison, or alternatively that it might be incorporated in a large Chapel School in the Norman style for which the architect and architectural historian Robert William Billings provided a design.

73 *The military prison built in 1840–2. As in the much larger prisons such as Pentonville which inspired it, rows of solitary cells on each floor open from a central galleried hall.*

Although the Chapel School idea was abandoned, the 1850s continued with a burst of activity and grand proposals initiated by the Inspector General of Fortifications on behalf of the War Office, and helped on locally by another senior Sapper officer, Lieutenant-Colonel Richard Moody. In 1853 the latter replaced the Main Guardhouse of around 1800 by a new one, an essay in a revived ancient Scottish style including gun-loops, within the much-reconstructed north flank of the sixteenth-century Spur. There were then plans, some by Billings, some by Moody, to refashion the North Barracks facing Crown Square (as the principal court was now called), perhaps making it into a chapel, and to erect a donjon-like armoury near St Margaret's Chapel. Most ambitiously, the architect Francis Dollman joined in by preparing designs for a château-like recasting of the whole north-western quarter of the Castle. During 1857 the roof was taken off the North Barracks in preparation for its remodelling, and in the next year Moody began a rebuilding of the wall above the Western Defences as a picturesque rampart of which only the first stage was completed. Work ended prematurely with public criticism that the Castle was being spoilt by an overzealous thirst for change, a reaction in the tradition of adverse comments by such men as Sir Walter Scott and Lord Cockburn on earlier military structures. None of the other schemes just listed was carried out, though there were to be many more proposals for new romantic buildings and inventive restorations, executed or unachieved.

While the imagination of engineers and architects was trying to conjure visions of former splendour, one of the most potent symbols of the turbulence and drama of the past disappeared almost unnoticed. With the retirement of the Commander-in-Chief in Scotland and Governor of Edinburgh Castle, Viscount Melville, in 1860, the office of Governor was allowed to lapse. For a long time there had been no tangible function for the office-bearer to perform.

CHAPTER SIX

Being and Becoming –
1860 to the present

Add glory to the past

The varied schemes of the 1850s and their different outcomes expressed a problem with several aspects (**74**). In terms of its contribution in new buildings and – until the previous decade – in alterations to old ones, the long domination of the military was seen as something of a disaster. This view was compounded by the universally low esteem into which the plainer and more functional kinds of Georgian architecture had sunk. As a consequence it was felt that one of the most spectacular sites in Europe lacked appropriately ancient-looking buildings – yet innovation might conflict with the authentic relics of the past. Another dimension of the problem was that, while the importance of the Castle was being increasingly recognized by public opinion, and was looked on sympathetically by individual military men, it was not really a function of the War Office to spend money on preserving historic buildings. A split in responsibility for the Castle opened in 1877 when St Margaret's Chapel along with 'Queen Mary's Rooms' in the Palace were given into the care of the Office of Works. The Office, which already looked after the 'Regalia Room' in the Palace and was responsible for the official who had immediate custody of the Crown Jewels, was in 1881 given charge of the first Ancient Monuments Act; and so its scattered holding in the stronghold came under the umbrella of ancient monumentry.

Late in 1883 the retired diplomat Lord Napier wrote to *The Scotsman* urging the restoration of the Great Hall, still divided up by the floors and partitions inserted in 1737 to make it into a more convenient barracks, and further altered for use as a military hospital since the beginning of the nineteenth century. Napier had just visited the Castle with Major Gore Booth of the Royal Engineers, who took an eager interest in his place of duty and who had explored several still discernible but little known features of the Hall, including its venerable timber roof. Gore Booth's enthusiasm for his investigations helped inspire a new wave of concern to beautify the buildings of the fortress. At first Gore Booth hoped that the authorities might be persuaded to undertake the task, but the War Office was lukewarm. He then turned to the Edinburgh publisher William Nelson, who had already offered financial aid if an appeal for funds were to be launched (**77**). In 1885 Nelson volunteered to pay for work on the Great Hall and the Portcullis Gate, together with the further restoration

74 (Above right) *The unexecuted proposal by David Bryce for a great tower near the summit of the Rock as a memorial to Prince Albert, 1864. It is the most accomplished of the many schemes produced around this time to try to make the Castle look more picturesque.*

75 (Below right) *The Castle's palisaded main entry, which had taken shape in Charles II's time, survived until 1886. This photograph was taken in the 1860s.*

of St Margaret's Chapel, as a personal enterprise. The idea was acceptable in principle to the military authorities, and Nelson chose Hippolyte Jean Blanc, a man of French origins settled in Scotland, as architect.

At the same time the Inspector General of Fortifications, Lieutenant-General Sir Andrew Clarke, had independently decided to improve the Castle with a new Entrance Gateway in the baronial style. The Gateway and its flanking ranges were to provide new accommodation for the guard with new detention cells (thus replacing the 1853 guardhouse extended in 1866, and now after a short active life destined to be turned into various kinds of store), together with a court-martial room on the upper floor above the gate itself. This military scheme was prepared in some secrecy in 1886, apparently for fear of the kind of adverse public reaction that Colonel Moody's projects had brought some thirty years earlier.

The Blanc–Nelson proposals on the other hand were freely publicized, and further opinions canvassed. There were conflicting views over St Margaret's Chapel, esteemed as one of the most precious and evocative buildings in Scotland. On the one hand Blanc wanted to enrich it with Romanesque detail, and the founding fathers of Scottish architectural history, David Macgibbon and Thomas Ross, heard of his proposals with approval. On the other hand the discoverer of the Chapel, Daniel Wilson, counselled restraint:

> The work of restoration of an ancient historical building such as this, ought to be carried out in the most conservative spirit. What is wanted is not a fine building, with all possible modern additions; but the original, or a facsimile of it in any effaced portions.

77 *The Edinburgh publisher William Nelson (1816–87) who sponsored romantic additions to the Portcullis Gate and the restoration of the Great Hall.*

It is a classic statement of a growing conservative position, expressing reservations shared by the Office of Works which now had charge of the chapel as an ancient monument; so Blanc's scheme hung fire.

The conflicting views on what might be done to the Chapel fitted into a contemporary British debate on ancient buildings. In Western Europe as well as Great Britain, many architects and those interested in architecture felt that the past might be imaginatively restored to its former glory, drawing where necessary on comparative material for detail and ornament, and a great deal of scholarship was devoted to seeking out a

76 *The Entrance Gateway designed and built in 1886–8, replacing the defences of the old main entry.*

variety of exemplars. A newer grouping in Britain, conspicuously led by William Morris, opposed 'restoration' in this permissive sense and advocated the caution voiced by Daniel Wilson: old buildings were seen as having attained an exemplary state of being, and it was wrong to try to make them become something different, for whatever worthy motives. The future ancient monuments policy of the Office of Works was to lie very firmly in this second camp.

Save for the case of St Margaret's Chapel, at Edinburgh Castle the restorers were to have the advantage. The Portcullis Gate scheme seems to have been accepted without demur, even though here Blanc's aim was restoration in an extreme form: to replace the plain and then much disliked eighteenth-century upper storey with its pitched slated roof by a completely new battlemented tower (78). Blanc put forward the idea in the belief that the gate stood on the site of David's Tower (the true site of the latter being lost to memory rather like St Margaret's Chapel) and so it could be restored to an appearance it might feasibly have had when built by David II. The composition was applauded for its good architectural style and picturesque effect on an important viewpoint of the Castle. It was to be called the 'Argyle Tower', in the belief that the ninth Earl of Argyle was imprisoned above the gate before his execution in 1685. This was the first work financed by Nelson to be executed, the contract being let in September 1886 with an optimistic three-months completion date. Externally, Blanc's contribution to the romantic past has the angle rounds, corbelled-out parapet, crow-stepped gables and stone-slabbed roof of late medieval Scottish architecture, with exotic wooden shutters closing the crenels of the parapet.

Inside the 'Argyle Tower', the upper room was built completely new in 1886–7. William Nelson vainly hoped that the Honours of Scotland would be brought here from the 'Crown Room' in the Palace, but in the event no enduring use has ever been found for the interior. Beneath the newly-created chamber is a vault

78 *In 1886–7 the architect Hippolyte Blanc added upper works to the sixteenth-century Portcullis Gate in the form of a tower, in the imagined style of the time of David II. This superimposed building, financed by William Nelson, was named the Argyle Tower.*

forming part of the fabric of the ancient gatehouse, clad in new masonry by Blanc but otherwise unaltered. It once housed the winding mechanism of the portcullis, and the portcullis slot is still visible in the floor. The vault was used as a prison, though there is no concrete evidence that Argyle was lodged here.

The Great Hall project (79) was briefly delayed while temporary accommodation was found for the hospital. The keys were handed over to Blanc in February 1887 and work started with Nelson canvassing the idea that it might become a National Armoury or military museum. In the summer of 1887 there must have seemed no limit to the possibilities for the transformation of the Castle. In July Nelson dined with Andrew Carnegie, hoping to direct some of the expatriate Scot's immense wealth to altering the 1796 New Barracks 'to make it decent architecturally ... with a castellated appearance given to it'. The dreams died with William Nelson on 10 September. His widow and trustees carried on with the Great Hall and in spite of difficulties with contractors finished it in 1891.

Blanc seems to have taken account of most of the structural evidence available to guide him in his work on the exterior of the Great Hall, though he did not stick closely to it, and went beyond any evidence in, for example, inserting a completely new gothic door towards its west end. Inside, nearly everything apart from the hammerbeam roof is part of the 1887–91 work (80). The great hooded fireplace in the east wall occupies an original fireplace position, but Blanc was responsible for the whole design of what exists, as he was also responsible for the conception of the panelling, the screen and gallery, and the other woodwork. He added

some new members to the roof and applied the surviving stencilled decoration to it. The result is not in several respects James IV's Great Hall, although it is an important late nineteenth-century interior in its own right. In a reflection of Nelson's wish, the War Office fitted up the Great Hall as an armoury, bringing weapons from Stirling Castle (much later the collection was replaced by the present display on loan from the Tower of London Armouries), and looked after both the Argyle Tower and the Hall until 1896, when both structures joined the other parts of the Castle accessible to the public in the care of the Office of Works.

The St Margaret's Chapel scheme was never revived and no other private schemes were started. The contribution of the Inspector General of Fortifications, the Entrance Gateway, had been finished, unapplauded, in 1888, after the preliminary demolition of a pattern of outer defences initiated in the time of Cromwell and Charles II. The Gateway had a 'rolling bridge', a kind of drawbridge that could be pulled back inside the entrance passage on cast-iron rollers. It was the last working drawbridge to be constructed in Scotland. Inside, there was accommodation for the guard, with a court-

79 William Nelson also financed Hippolyte Blanc's restoration of the Great Hall, begun in 1887 and completed after Nelson's death in 1891. This view from the principal courtyard, 'Crown Square', shows the reworked parapet; windows that Blanc refashioned to be wider than the originals; and a door that is entirely Blanc's (see also 25).

martial room on the upper floor and detention cells in the angled south wing. The Baronial detail of the gateway exterior was seen as poor and unscholarly at the time, and has not been commended since.

In 1893 plans were prepared by E. Ingress Bell, a consulting architect to the War Office, to demolish William Skinner's 1748 magazine and to remodel his 1753–4 Ordnance Stores as a modern military hospital (**81**), and the works completed in 1897 gave the buildings the form which they have today. The stone sentry boxes constructed in the mid-eighteenth century were moved sideways to make room for the kitchen attached to the north block. The latter was redesigned and raised a storey in height with added wings, in an early seventeenth-century style more effective as seen from the courtyard than from Princes Street. The changes to the south block were much less drastic, preserving the arches of the storehouse on the ground floor. The hospital is the tailpiece to this intensive endeavour to make the Castle conform better to the romantic historical awareness of the nineteenth century.

80 *The interior of the Great Hall is Hippolyte Blanc's conception in his work of 1887–91 save for the hammerbeam roof, altered by Blanc but essentially of the early 1500s. The enriched neo-medieval panelling and the hooded fireplace are noteworthy in a design that has an important place among late Victorian restorations. William Nelson thought that after its restoration the Great Hall might become an armoury, and in fact it has been used to display weapons since the 1890s. The collection shown here is on long loan from the Tower of London.*

Ancient monument

In 1905 care of all the Castle's buildings and fortifications was transferred from the War Office to the Office of Works, so that the whole fortress might be looked after as an ancient monument, replacing the patchwork of custody that had evolved. The Army reserved special rights in the parts which it still used, and proposals were still on the table for further change, notably a new Officers' Mess on Mills Mount. Nothing was done, however, for the thinking of the War Office was moving away from long-term occupation of the Castle, favouring instead a new and more conveniently planned barracks in the Edinburgh suburbs.

81 Designs were made in 1893 by E. Ingress Bell to refashion the mid-eighteenth-century twin Ordnance Stores as a military hospital (demolishing the magazine that lay between them). The work was carried out, with some changes to Bell's scheme, in 1897.

82 Redford Barracks, built in the suburbs of Edinburgh between 1909 and 1915, became the new home of the Castle's garrison after the First World War.

Redford Barracks was begun in 1909, and the last of its widely spreading blocks were still under construction when war broke out in 1914 (**82**).

A few years earlier another discovery had been made of a renowned building thought to be lost. In the previous century, while he was engaged on the restoration of the Great Hall, the architect Hippolyte Blanc had found an embrasure in part of the confusing cellarage beneath the gun platform of the Half-Moon. He thought that it might possibly belong to David's Tower, but confirmation of Blanc's intuition was deferred for two decades. In 1912 three members of the recently created and elaborately named Royal Commission on the Ancient and Historical Monuments and Constructions of Scotland, including the distinguished architect and architectural historian Thomas Ross, made the same inference. The site was explored and then cleared out by the Office of Works, firmly identifying the remains of the late fourteenth-century tower shattered in the siege of 1573. The masonry of David's Tower, together with that of the mid-sixteenth-century gun emplacement commanding the Castle Hill immediately to the north, was subsequently made good, and for some time visitors to the Castle were able to see these structures. (They have now been inaccessible for many years, but Historic Scotland is planning to open them again.)

Intensive use of the Castle was resumed for the duration of the First World War (83). While it was in progress the Castle's ancient function as a State prison was revived. In August 1916 the Marxist revolutionary John Maclean, who subsequently founded the Workers' Republican

83 Troops drawn up on the Esplanade in front of the Castle during the First World War.

Party with the aim of establishing a communist republic of Scotland, was imprisoned there for making speeches contravening the Defence of the Realm Act. He was confined in the Victorian military prison with David Kirkwood and others of the extreme left. The prison was closed down in 1923, by which time the Edinburgh garrison had been concentrated at Redford.

Planning had by then already begun to convert the North Barracks in Crown Square into a memorial to the Scottish dead of the Great War. The final drawings were made late in 1924 by Sir Robert Lorimer, and the War Memorial was opened by the Prince of Wales (later Edward VIII) on 14 July 1927 (84). Lorimer added a five-sided apse to the north which ornately dominates the citadel-summit. He also built on a porch on the opposite side, towards the square. The massing of the block was otherwise retained, for its origin as soldiers' quarters was part of the symbolism. The exterior of the whole was richly worked to designs by Lorimer of

84 *The opening of the Scottish National War Memorial by the Prince of Wales (later Edward VIII) on 14 July 1927.*

variations on ancient Scottish architectural detail, and elaborated inside and out by a team of artists and craftsmen.

The exterior of the Memorial carries sculpture idealizing the 'just war'. On the front towards Crown Square, to the left of the porch are: Courage, a mailed figure with sword and shield; Peace, a female with doves; and a Cross of Sacrifice between the windows. To the right of the porch are: Justice blindfolded with scales and sword; Mercy, a warrior with a child; and a second Cross of Sacrifice. The keystone of the porch door is carved with a winged and flaming heart to typify love, courage and sacrifice. Above the door is a figure rising from a phoenix,

symbolizing the survival of the spirit (the images were given these meanings by the scheme's originators). The rest of the exterior continues the theme.

Inside there first came the Hall of the Regiments, or the Hall of Honour as it is now called, with the Rolls of Honour of the regiments. The hall has a concrete vault, so designed by Lorimer to prevent outward thrust on the walls of the old barrack building, too thin to carry a vault in stone. Beneath the vault is a frieze of battle honours. The names of the dead of the Second World War were incorporated into the Rolls of Honour, and there have also been added the names of those who have died in conflicts since 1945, for the commemorative purpose of the Memorial continues up to the present day. From the hall opens the Shrine in the apse, with a steel casket containing a complete Scottish roll of honour, and a spectacular figure of St Michael

85 *The Scottish National War Memorial was remodelled by Sir Robert Lorimer from an eighteenth-century barracks. Work began in 1924. Ornamental detail was added to the existing building which was extended northwards by an elaborately worked apse to contain the Shrine.*

armed, suspended from the central boss of the apse's vault.

The representational art of the interior takes in two quite separate impressions of the 1914–18 war. One is a simple record of war scenes, of people and machines, a recollection in tranquillity of a hideous conflict. Among Douglas Strachan's stained-glass windows in the hall (86), one shows a heavy gun, a soldier hurling a grenade, a flame-thrower, a machine-gun, an armoured car, two tanks, a trench-cutting machine, and sappers building a bridge. The calm design and modelling of the bronze friezes

in the shrine, by Alice and Morris Meredith-Williams, show the variously uniformed men and women who fought, or who supported the struggle. The other impression is the heightened imagery in Strachan's windows for the Shrine, of the conflict seen as the battle of Armageddon, the war to end war. The central window includes Peace seated with the corpse of War between her knees. The windows to the left show the beginnings of human strife with Cain and Abel. The windows to the right draw on the Book of Revelation, with the white horse and its rider called Faithful and True, followed by the armies of heaven upon white horses. The rider called Faithful and True wears a swastika on his cloak, covering his upper arm. The ancient symbol of good fortune had not then acquired new meanings.

The Duke of Atholl who chaired the committee for the War Memorial also proposed a

86 *The Scottish National War Memorial: Great War tanks in stained glass.*

War Museum of the 1914–18 war, almost as it were as an annexe to the former. The idea evolved into a museum taking in material from a much longer time-span of the Scottish land and sea services, and in 1933 the Naval and Military Museum was opened in the Queen Anne Barracks, which had been internally gutted to accommodate the exhibits of uniforms and weapons, although its very plain elevations were left largely unaltered.

Now was the lowest ebb of active military use of the Castle. The Hospital was still functioning, but the huge fabric of the 1796–9 New Barracks was normally only occupied by a small guard party sent from Redford, the subaltern in command living uncomfortably in an old-fashioned flat on the top floor of the block. It was being seriously considered whether the New Barracks might be partly taken down and the remaining structure remodelled, or whether it might even be demolished altogether. In less than a century since the first military quarters had been relinquished, almost the whole of the fortress had become a memorial with a number of facets reflecting the recent or remote past. It was as a gesture to past Scottish glory that statues of William Wallace and King Robert I (the Bruce) (see **18**) were placed in niches in the Victorian Entrance Gateway in 1929, to commemorate the six hundredth anniversary of Robert's death – though Wallace had no associations with the Castle, and Bruce's contribution to the story was to order the destruction of the defences after the stronghold had been daringly captured by his henchmen. And as another token of respect for the past, the office of Governor was re-established in 1935, with purely honorary duties.

During the Second World War the Army came back again in strength to use the Castle, and in 1942, as a precaution against air attack, the Honours of Scotland were buried in David's Tower – an appropriate site, for the Treasury seems to have been located there in ancient times. After hostilities ended there was a brief revival of an old function. The Headquarters of Scottish Command had to be moved from the *Scotsman* building on North Bridge in Edinburgh when the accommodation there was de-requisitioned, and it was brought into the now-empty Hospital for several years until the completion of the new Headquarters at Craigiehall House. The Operations Room in the Hospital survived until 1958.

Meanwhile the military presence in the postwar years was making a novel contribution to the Edinburgh scene. When the city held its first International Festival in August and September 1947, the Army contributed an evening military display on the Esplanade. It was a simply-staged affair with the march and countermarch of pipes and drums, and it was an immediate success. Growing in scale, and unlike the rest of the

Festival running at a profit, the Tattoo has been repeated ever since on the same site against the most dramatic backdrop of any such production anywhere. The large audiences require massive tiered constructions of temporary purpose-designed scaffolding (see **90**), which take some time to erect and dismantle; and so during the summer and autumn the Castle is extended eastward by a surreal barbican of tubular framework.

On top of the Rock, the Naval and Military Museum, taking in Royal Air Force material, was re-opened in 1949 as the Scottish United Services Museum. Its displays were then extended into the first floor of the Palace, the one-time Royal Apartment being prosaically referred to by the museum authorities as the 'East Galleries'. Individual museums were developed by the Royal Scots, who had been allocated the Castle as their permanent regimental depot in 1881, and by the Royal Scots Greys. Also during the post-war period, the Great Hall acquired an active employment for the first time since its Victorian restoration, as a setting for State banquets and other government functions. This use increased, notably after limited administrative responsibility for the care of the Castle and ancient monuments in general passed to the Scottish Office in 1969.

The long chronicle of repair continued from the beginning of the century under the Office of Works and the variously named departments which succeeded it. Aside from the substantial adaptations that have been described, operations were for the most part confined to conservative preservation. There were, however, exceptions, such as the replacement of the mid-nineteenth-century Norman revival door-piece of St Margaret's Chapel by an unostentatious design by the Office of Works architect John Wilson Paterson in 1939: an instance of the Office's self-effacing philosophy which contrasted sharply with the special case of the War Memorial scheme of the previous decade.

More recently, a striking undertaking of preservation was prompted by the failing

87 *The National Thanksgiving, 24 June 1953, when the Scottish Regalia were brought before the Queen in St Giles Cathedral. Here Sir Thomas Innes of Learney, Lyon King of Arms, bears the Crown from the Castle.*

margins of the geological formation on which the Castle stands. The volcanic rock is very hard but its structure of vertical columns makes exposed sections liable to split off in fragments. The process of very slow disintegration has always been a characteristic of the site. It emerged as a substantial safety problem after the formation of Johnston Terrace and the railway beneath the south and north crags respectively, and in the 1960s it had become obvious that cementing or removal of pieces of loose rock was no longer an adequate response. After a geological survey, a specialist contractor carried out the

first phase of 'rock-bolting' in 1968: drilling through the loose outer columns of rock to the stable core, inserting and fixing steel bolts some 10m (33ft) long, and embedding the whole in waterproof cement. The rock-bolting programme went on for more than a decade and its scaffolds on the precipices became a familiar feature to the citizens and a surprise to visitors.

In April 1979, as part of the interim arrangements anticipating the setting up of a Scottish Assembly, several Scottish elements of Whitehall-run government departments were taken into the Scottish Office for what was seen as a 'bed-and-breakfast' stay before final transfer to the control of the Assembly. Among them was the organization that looked after ancient monuments including Edinburgh Castle. The Assembly was not set up as planned, but the interim arrangements stuck. The responsibility for the Castle – over the previous decade awkwardly divided – therefore fell wholly to the Secretary of State for Scotland. The transfer was not to be just a footnote in the history of administration: it was to have significant consequences for separate developments in Scotland and in England.

Welcome

Late in 1979 a new 'Ancient Monuments and Archaeological Areas Act' covering the whole of Great Britain was passed to replace earlier legislation. Its main endeavour was to give more bite to the regulations, giving particular attention to tightening and enlarging the possible scope of archaeological controls. The concerns which through the next decade were to dominate thinking and action at places open to the public run by government appear only fleetingly, in a brief paragraph empowering the Secretary of State and local authorities to provide facilities, information and services at ancient monuments.

Outside the rather enclosed world of statute, the forces that were to change the future of ancient monuments in Britain open to visitors, and pre-eminently the few places with large or, like Edinburgh Castle, very large numbers of visitors, had been gathering for a long time. The forerunners from the end of the 1940s were great country houses in England, and a decade or so later more and more places were opening their doors and bringing in revenues that made a real contribution to costs of upkeep. Operating with a clear awareness of the significance of the new industry of tourism, owners promoted their 'visitor attractions' with growing ease in a quasi-commercial world new to the scholarly field of architectural history. In the 1970s Visitor Centres – a term recently coined – were opened as an added attraction for people, who then bought souvenirs at associated shops to supplement admission charges. The staff of the visitor attractions were trained to go out of their way to make people, seen as valued customers, feel welcome.

The new values did not visibly impinge upon, and some of its emphases seemed rather alien to, the compartment of ancient monuments. Among these in Scotland, Edinburgh Castle, as the place with by far the highest visitor numbers, became a focus of attention in letters to Ministers and in the press. A campaign in *The Scotsman* and the *Edinburgh Evening News* criticized at length inadequate facilities there to receive and look after visitors. Those in the Scottish Office were certainly not complacent about the position, but there were real difficulties in setting about the drastic changes needed. The ancient monuments organization had developed in the civil service, with the traditional virtues and limitations of that body: detached, objective, circumscribed by strict financial mechanisms and manpower controls. It was only latterly that the Treasury had allowed that visitor income might be retained to defray the annual vote of funds – previously all income had to be handed over to the Treasury, which was scarcely an incentive to increase revenue from ancient monuments. On manpower, any staff that might be proposed to strengthen visitor services, as it might be a shop assistant, would have to be counted against the global Scottish Office complement. In general, too, the organization had developed with a very strong professional and works weighting that targeted effectively on preservation, but had no slack and limited spontaneous inclination to look after visitors with an equal sense of mission, let alone to think of income potential in the perspectives of the market place.

Pressure for changed approaches grew as Ministers south of the Border became concerned over falling visitor numbers at some much-frequented ancient monuments, as against increases in the private sector. In 1984 a new public body governed by commissioners, called English Heritage, was created to succeed the old organization in England. At the same time Scotland took the more restricted step of setting up a new Historic Buildings and Monuments Directorate still firmly within the Scottish Office structure but, it was hoped, better able to respond to new demands and priorities, not least in providing for visitors.

One of the new Scottish Director's first tasks was to get a blueprint for the future of Edinburgh Castle. The Boys Jarvis Partnership, a Glasgow firm of architects, was successful in its tender for the job and published its report in 1986 (see **91**). A number of themes for visitors from the stronghold's long history were explored, and most of these were to be, and are being, followed up. But one recommendation was so striking and innovatory that it diverted public and press attention from the rest: to make permanent provision for

the Tattoo and other events that might be staged on the Esplanade by creating a seated amphitheatre there (see **91**). The one-time fortress, royal seat, arsenal and chief barracks would now be architecturally placarded as a major place of entertainment and spectacle.

The shock of the new was too much for public opinion and the idea was not pursued. It was, however, significant as an indicator that attitudes to change were not everywhere rigid, and also because linked to the Esplanade scheme was a lightly-sketched idea that was to be elaborated and carried out with some unexpected consequences. A long-standing awkwardness inside the Castle had been the sharing of the narrow and tortuous route up from the Entrance Gate between visitors to the ancient monument and

88 *Stands being put up on the Castle Esplanade for the Edinburgh Festival Tattoo in 1958.*

89 *The first shop in the Castle was opened in 1982 in the Mills Mount Cart Shed.*

War Memorial and vehicles servicing the Army units, the works staff, the museum, and, since 1982, a shop in the Mills Mount Cart Shed (**89**). Continuous efforts to limit numbers and hours of passage of vehicles were never very successful. The Boys Jarvis report proposed to 'pedestrianize' the route, diverting vehicles along the north side of the proposed Esplanade amphitheatre, across the north end of the ditch by a late-Victorian service-access bridge, and inside the Castle by a tunnel cut on a line taking it under St Margaret's Chapel and issuing beyond the Cart Shed shop.

As far as the authors of the report were concerned the tunnel would have been desirable rather than essential with the envisaged amphitheatre in place: their overall proposals for a new shop and restaurant would certainly generate an appreciable amount of service traffic but, since these facilities were to be located under the amphitheatre seating, the traffic would not enter the Castle. The decision not to proceed with the Esplanade ideas substantially strengthened arguments for the tunnel in spite of its high cost. The shop and restaurant would now have to be contrived inside the Castle, and the sites provisionally chosen for them – the 1853 Guardhouse and the Mills Mount Cart Shed – actually lay over the drafted line of the tunnel and so could be serviced directly from it. But before a revised blueprint might be settled on, agreement had to be reached between the Army, the Directorate and the Museum on new zones of occupation for each to replace the patchwork quilt of use that had haphazardly developed in the past. This done, a complicated rolling programme of work was set in motion in 1988 and is still going on.

The archaeological preliminaries to the tunnel project were among the earliest elements in the programme. As was discussed in the first chapter, only in the central section was the tunnel proper to be bored through the basalt. To west and east were lengths of 'cut-and-cover', deep trenches excavated then revetted and covered with concrete. These operations would disturb archaeology and so the preliminary examinations already described were commissioned. The excavations at the west end in front of the Mills Mount Cart Shed, with their discoveries from prehistory and the Roman age, were very much in the public eye and became quite a showpiece for their duration. The excavations at the east end were less conspicuously inside the buildings, particularly the 1853 Guardhouse. The latter were immediately followed by the construction of a much bigger new shop in and beyond the Guardhouse with its own tunnel access, while the central tunnel section through the Rock was begun. In July 1990 this underground access to the Castle interior was opened to traffic (**92**), and the ancient route up from the Entrance Gate became a pedestrian walkway (**93**). The shop was decanted from the Cart Shed to the new site soon afterwards and work began to transform and extend the Cart Shed as a restaurant. The extension (**94**), above the west mouth of the tunnel, was designed by an Edinburgh firm of architects, Robert Matthew, Johnson-Marshall and Partners.

While all this was in progress there was another change in the Directorate's status. The Historic Buildings and Monuments Directorate had for some time used 'Historic Scotland' for its publicity as a less unwieldy name. In April 1991 the latter became the formal title of a new Executive Agency formed from the Directorate. With extra independence within the Scottish Office, Historic Scotland was given more scope for commercial operations as well as more appropriate finance and personnel responsibilities.

Works to improve on-site presentation at the Castle had been going on for several years. The first significant element, as far back as 1984, took in new displays in the vaults below the Great Hall, with costume figures in the 'French Prisons', and Mons Meg now brought into an adjoining vault – for its better protection – from the open-air site the gun had occupied since 1829. The 1842 military prison was then made accessible and explained; and a minor exhibition of objects found in the archaeological excavations from 1988 was put into the ground floor of the Palace – an initial list that begins to indicate the range that had to be covered. The first really large presentation scheme, however, had to await the transfer of the Scottish United Services

90 Visitors and buses on the Esplanade in 1985, with sophisticated Tattoo stands.

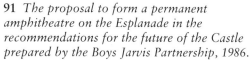

SCHEME 4   Arena with seating, and no tour buses near Esplanade, only shuttle buses from Holyrood Car Park.

91 *The proposal to form a permanent amphitheatre on the Esplanade in the recommendations for the future of the Castle prepared by the Boys Jarvis Partnership, 1986.*

Museum from the first floor of the Palace as part of the establishment of coherent zones of occupation for the users of the Castle. In 1991–2 the evacuated rooms in the Palace were closely examined for evidence that might throw light on the enigmatic architectural history of the building, before operations began for a new exhibition on the subject of the Royal Line and the Honours of Scotland, which opened in 1993 (**95**). More themes such as the Castle as Prison and the Castle as Garrison are being worked on for other locations.

This wide-ranging programme triggered by the requirement to pay very much better attention to visitors, either now carried out or planned for the future, will make little external change to the Castle. The roof of part of the 1990 shop is just visible from the neighbouring

terrain, though more in the public gaze is the restaurant extension to the Mills Mount Cart Shed, completed and opened in June 1992. The playful detail of the new design's gable and dormers replace the view of a high blank stone wall as seen from Princes Street.

The other uses of the Castle go on as before. The Tattoo continues its annual success and dominates the summer scene by its vast pattern of scaffolding. The Army, some of its accommodation relocated, provides both a living sense of long history with its traditionally-uniformed sentries at the Entrance Gate, and an uncomfortable reminder of today's need for security against terrorism with night-time guards and

92 (Above right) *The tunnel through the Castle Rock is opened by the Minister, Lord James Douglas-Hamilton, in July 1990.*

93 (Below right) *'Pedestrianized' access for visitors into the Castle became possible after the opening of the tunnel in 1990: the photograph shows a crowd near Portcullis Gate.*

94 (Above left) *The Castle restaurant in the Mills Mount Cart Shed was extended to the west by a new building completed in 1992.*

95 (Below left) *Part of the exhibition of the Honours of Scotland and the Royal line, opened in the Castle's Palace by Her Majesty the Queen in 1993. The tableau shows the presentation of the Sword, a gift from Pope Julius II, to James IV in 1507.*

patrols in camouflage fatigues. The Scottish National War Memorial goes on unchanged as a place of pilgrimage. The once-scattered Scottish United Services Museum is coming together into its now compact holding of the ex-Hospital. And sumptuous State functions continue, such as the lunch for Europe's leaders when the European Council met in Edinburgh in December 1992 (**96**).

96 *The European Council at Edinburgh: lunch at the Castle, 11 December 1992. The Prime Minister of the United Kingdom, John Major, is host as President of the Council at that time. The group of the European Community's heads is standing in front of the fireplace at the east end of the Great Hall.*

Looking at the Castle Today

The most familiar impressions of the Castle, either viewing it at a distance from Princes Street, or approaching and entering the stronghold from the Castle Hill, immediately begin to illustrate the long and complicated story, the transformation and renewal of buildings and functions, which I have attempted to tell.

97 *This aerial photograph of Edinburgh Castle today shows the fortifications and buildings identified and briefly discussed in the following two pages. (See also the drawing on p. 136.)*

The approach is over the Esplanade **A**, made up with a regular surface as parade ground for soldiers and promenade for citizens, and given its present form in the 1820s. Then one crosses the Ditch to the Victorian Entrance Gate **B**; these represent the final state of the works at the Castle's most vulnerable approach, succeeding a catalogue of defensive ideas that seems to go back to prehistoric times. Once inside the Castle a long winding ascent **C** begins with to the left a Guardhouse of 1853 now transformed into the gift shop, through the eighteenth-century Inner Barrier to the formidable obstacle of the Portcullis Gate **D**, constructed after the great siege of 1573 with decorative upper works added in 1886–7.

The broad cobbled roadway **E** beyond the Gate passes the foundations of another guardhouse of about 1800 on the left, while on the right (above earlier flanking works) are gun positions of George II's garrison, part of a replanning of the defences carried out in 1730–7 when General Wade was Commander-in-Chief in Scotland. The 1730s perimeter, extending round the rest of the northern side **EF**, and then along the western side of the Rock, is dramatically seen from Princes Street rising and falling above the crags.

From both Princes Street and the Castle's approach and entry, the scene is crowned by the fortifications and buildings of the citadel-like summit of the Rock. The Half-Moon Battery **G** was first devised, and the Forewall Battery **H** remodelled, after the 1573 siege. Nearby, quite conspicuous although plain and small in scale, is the oldest standing building in the Castle, the twelfth-century St Margaret's Chapel **J**. Its original purpose forgotten, it was for a long time part of the Gunner's establishment – as a reminder of that establishment, the rectangular

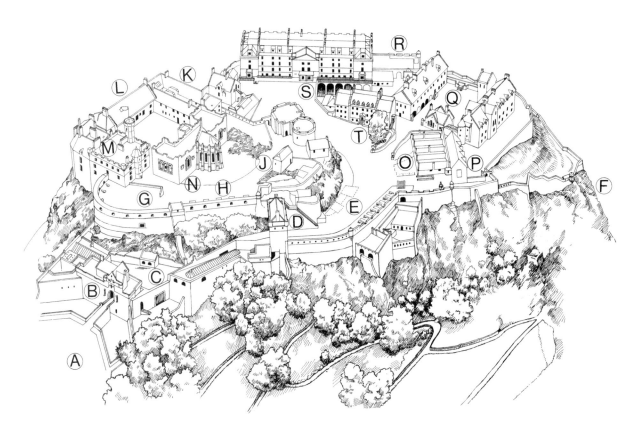

Shot and Shell Yard survives nearby, converted into a reservoir (with a purpose-built circular battlemented reservoir beside it). St Margaret's Chapel was once at the focus of the royal life of the Castle; but this moved to the south as a new principal courtyard took shape around 1500. Now called Crown Square, the courtyard is surrounded by an extraordinary assemblage of buildings **KLMN**. All of them have fascinating stories of change.

To the west, the rectangle of the Queen Anne Building **K** was built for garrison officers, the Castle minister, and gunners, and is among the oldest structures in Britain purpose-built for army residential use. Its vaulted substructure is much older, part of the Gunhouse mentioned in 1498. The vaults are entered from Dury's Battery, one of the Queen Anne improvements to the defences. Nearby is the early Victorian military prison – the vaults themselves had been a very different kind of place of confinement, part of the prison of war of the later eighteenth and early nineteenth centuries, and the once so-called 'French Prisons' (there were captives of other nationalities crammed in too) extend also under the southern building **L**, the Great Hall. In the furthest vault is displayed the mighty bombard Mons Meg, made in 1449. The Great Hall above was completed for James IV, and is seen today adorned internally by a major late Victorian restoration which swept away Georgian alterations as barracks and military hospital.

The Palace **M** occupies the east side of the courtyard. Its nucleus dates back to the 1430s and the future James VI of Scotland and I of England was born in the Royal Lodging here in 1566. When James revisited his northern kingdom in 1617 the Palace was reconstructed for him to the form it has today. For centuries the Crown Jewels, the Honours of Scotland, have been kept here, and they figure conspicuously in an exhibition in the Palace opened in 1993. Finally, on the north side is the richly decorated Scottish National War Memorial **N**, originally designed to commemorate the dead of the 1914–

18 Great War. A long line of buildings has stood on the site: barracks, the Munition House and a succession of churches which could go back as far as the seventh century AD.

The place where the earliest occupation has been established, however, lies below the summit to the west. The area in front of the 1746 Cart Shed **O** (later turned into a barracks and now part of the Castle restaurant) on Mills Mount was excavated at an early stage of the 1988–91 work in advance of the service tunnel, and revealed positive evidence that prehistoric man lived on the Rock. Behind the remarkably-surviving shed is the western part of the restaurant which is the newest building **P** in the Castle. From Mills Mount one may also visit the collections of the Scottish United Services Museum, located in the 1897 military Hospital fashioned from one of a pair of George II Ordnance Stores **Q**.

From the western end of Princes Street and the gardens, the ex-Hospital is one of the most dominant buildings in the Castle, rising above two tiers of ramparts: the lower one the 1730s defensive line already mentioned, with also an upper Victorian ornamental fortification which was never finished. More serious works are resumed with the early eighteenth-century Butts Battery **R**, and then a most imposing view of the huge New Barracks of 1796–9 **S**. The rest of the circuit beyond the walls is well worth following, by King's Stables Road and the Grassmarket, or by Johnston Terrace, with precipices capped by the Queen Anne Building, the Great Hall, the Palace, and then the Half-Moon, looking more like architectural fiction than reality.

Inside the stronghold again, the broad cobbled roadway ascending from Mills Mount allows the appreciation at close quarters of the New Barracks and the distinguished Governor's House **T** finished in 1742. In this quarter of the Castle there is clustered a remarkable and most varied grouping of Georgian military architecture, emphasizing one of the many themes of the story.

Further Reading

The report on the 1988–91 archaeological excavations at the Castle has not yet been published. It will appear as a Society of Antiquaries of Scotland monograph: Stephen Driscoll and Peter Yeoman, *Excavations at Edinburgh Castle, 1988–91*. I have used material from its draft mostly for my first chapter, but the report will reflect the variety of knowledge recovered relating to the story of the Rock and the Castle up to the nineteenth century.

The best recent account of the surviving architecture of the Castle, with a historical introduction, is in the Buildings of Scotland volume on *Edinburgh* by John Gifford, Colin McWilliam and David Walker, with Christopher Wilson, Penguin Books 1984. The Royal Commission on the Ancient and Historical Monuments' *Inventory of Edinburgh*, HMSO Edinburgh 1945, gives very full descriptions of older structures but progressively dries up after 1707. Treatments worth looking at to show earlier emphases include the entries in volume I of David McGibbon and Thomas Ross, *The Castellated and Domestic Architecture of Scotland*, Edinburgh 1887–92 and Daniel Wilson, *Memorials of Edinburgh in the Olden Time*, Edinburgh 1848.

On specific contents of the Castle, Charles Burnett and Christopher Tabraham, *The Honours of Scotland, the story of the Scottish Crown Jewels*, Edinburgh 1993, gives an excellent picture of the subject.

Its scale and its long complicated history have left Edinburgh Castle without any closely relevant peer group in Scotland, though further afield the Tower of London (Geoffrey Parnell, *The English Heritage Book of the Tower of London*, Batsford 1993) and – at first sight a very exotic linkage with its huge scale, superlative architecture and opulence – the Moscow Kremlin as national fortress-palace-arsenal-treasury (for instance, Irina Rodimtseva, *The Moscow Kremlin*, Aurora Art Publishers, Leningrad 1987) offer stimulating comparisons. Nearer home, Stirling Castle is closest to our subject, and there Historic Scotland's guidebook is a good introduction. The wider picture is given (in increasing detail of treatment) in Christopher Tabraham's *Scottish Castles*, HMSO Edinburgh 1990, John Dunbar's *The Architecture of Scotland*, Batsford 1978, and Stewart Cruden's *The Scottish Castle*, Edinburgh 1960.

As background to the early narrative of the Castle Rock, the following books and articles will be useful. On the geology, George P. Black, *Arthur's Seat, a History of Edinburgh's Volcano*, Oliver and Boyd, Edinburgh and London, 1966, enlarges Colin MacFadyen's opening section here. On relevant prehistory, the essays in A.L.E. Rivet, *The Iron Age in Northern Britain*, Edinburgh 1966 still give, I think, the best comprehensive view, supplemented by the summary in J.S. Rideout and others, *Hillforts of Southern Scotland*, Historic Scotland 1992; and for the period of Roman influence David J. Breeze, *The Northern Frontiers of Roman Britain*, Batsford, London 1982 (paperback edition 1993). For the 'Dark Ages' and the early Middle Ages, there are Charles Thomas, *Celtic Britain*, London 1986, and A.P. Smyth, *Warlords and Holy Men, Scotland 80–1000*, London 1984, as well as, specifically, Kenneth Hurlstone Jackson, *The Gododdin*, Edinburgh 1969,

Later, the story of the Castle inescapably brings in a host of references to Scottish history generally. Perhaps I might confine myself to recommending Michael Lynch, *Scotland: a New History*, London 1991, and the four volumes of *The Edinburgh History of Scotland* edited by Gordon Donaldson, 1968–75. From the references given in these one may branch out to explore particular aspects.

For the mainstream development of artillery fortification, a concise well-illustrated outline is given in Bruce W. Fry, '*An appearance of strength*': *The Fortifications of Louisbourg*, Parks Canada Ottawa 1984. For the rest of the military and post-military story, however, there are so far only scattered published sources, some of them rather tangential, such as J.B. Salmond, *Wade in Scotland*, 1934. Much of the military pattern has to be built up from documents and drawings – the Board of Ordnance collections of drawings, which may be consulted in the National Library of Scotland, and the British Library give a memorable flavour to the subject – though for comparison there is a wealth of illustration of military buildings especially of barracks, in *Deserted Bastions: Historic Naval and Military Architecture*, ed. Marianne Watson-Smyth, SAVE Britain's Heritage 1993 (the report published to accompany an exhibition). Similarly, the varied aims and enthusiasms of the nineteenth-century lack overview publication; one notices for example the lack of a historical treatment on the subject of restoration.

Glossary

Architectural Terms

apse A semicircular or polygonal extension of a major compartment of a building, especially at the east end of a church.

aumbry A cupboard, especially a recess in an interior wall of a building; in a church used for the sacramental vessels.

cartouche An ornamental tablet with a frame, often surrounding an inscription or device of arms.

corbel A block of stone, often decorated, projecting from a wall as a support for a feature – such as masonry, floor joists, or main structural roof timbers – on its upper surface.

crenel One of the indentations or embrasures of a battlemented parapet.

crow-step Stones set with the appearance of steps to form the sloping sides of a gable.

hammerbeam roof A timber roof ingeniously designed without cross-ties to give an open and spacious appearance; essential supports in the design are the short timbers or hammerbeams projecting from the inner faces of the wallheads.

mullion A vertical bar usually of stone dividing the lights of a window; a horizontal bar is a **transom**.

nook-shaft A small column set into an angle of masonry, especially at the sides of a door or window.

ogee A continuous double curve, convex above and concave below; an ogee arch made up of two such opposed curves is a characteristic form in gothic architecture.

quoin Dressed stones at the exterior angles of a building.

string-course A band or course of stone projecting slightly from the face of a wall.

transom See **mullion**.

Artillery Names

Different types and sizes of early gunpowder weapons were defined by a considerable variety of names. Among the earliest, and tending to be the biggest, were wrought-iron **bombards**, of which Mons Meg is an extra-large specimen; the name probably has a long descent from a Greek word meaning 'booming'. There were several sizes of **cannon**, of cast bronze, or later cast iron; the name coming prosaically from Italian 'big tube' might be used generally for any piece that had to be specially mounted to fire it, but also in a narrow sense for very big guns with bores from about 215mm (a 'great cannon') down to 170mm. Several names evoked more vivid images. Some carried the sense of evil associated with snakes, like **culverins** (ultimately from Latin *coluber* a snake) or **serpentines**; both were first used for long-barrelled wrought iron pieces of 60–40mm bore, but the former came to mean long-barrelled and therefore long-range heavy cast bronze guns with bores just smaller than cannon, the largest or 'great culverin' being about 135mm. Some were named after sportsmen's birds renowned for their swift destructive power, **falcons** (and in England **sakers**); all were cast bronze weapons, falcons between 65 and 40mm, sakers rather larger. Other names were not coded: Mons Meg was referred to as a 'great iron **murderer**', and on a much smaller scale there were wrought iron breech-loading **cut-throats**.

The vocabulary of the earlier catapults and other throwing-engines was less picturesque; the name of the huge counterpoise stone-throwing machines or **trébuchets** survives in France to describe – on a miniature scale in comparison – a precision balance.

Index

(Numbers in **bold** indicate illustrations)